THE SELECTED POETRY OF

Hayden Carruth

jetty
C
page
76
groves of
nerve

Other Books by Hayden Carruth

POETRY
The Crow and the Heart
Journey to a Known Place
The Norfolk Poems
North Winter
Nothing for Tigers
Contra Mortem
The Clay Hill Anthology
For You
From Snow and Rock, from Chaos
Dark World
The Bloomingdale Papers
Loneliness
Aura
Brothers, I Loved You All
The Mythology of Dark and Light
The Sleeping Beauty
If You Call This Cry a Song
Asphalt Georgics
The Oldest Killed Lake in North America
Lighter Than Air Craft

FICTION
Appendix A

CRITICISM
After the Stranger
Working Papers
Effluences from the Sacred Caves

ANTHOLOGIES
The Voice That Is Great Within Us
The Bird/Poem Book

THE SELECTED POETRY OF

Hayden Carruth

Foreword by Galway Kinnell

COLLIER BOOKS

Macmillan Publishing Company

New York

COLLIER MACMILLAN PUBLISHERS

London

Copyright © 1985 by Hayden Carruth

All rights reserved. No part of this book may be reproduced or transmitted in any form or by any means, electronic or mechanical, including photocopying, recording or by any information storage and retrieval system, without permission in writing from the Publisher.

Macmillan Publishing Company
866 Third Avenue, New York, N.Y. 10022
Collier Macmillan Canada, Inc.

Library of Congress Cataloging-in-Publication Data
Carruth, Hayden, 1921-
The selected poetry of Hayden Carruth.
I. Title.
PS3505.A77594A6   1985   811'.52   85-22389
ISBN 0-02-069310-9

The Selected Poetry of Hayden Carruth is also available in a hardcover edition from Macmillan Publishing Company.

10   9   8   7   6   5   4   3   2   1

Designed by Jack Meserole

Printed in the United States of America

Permission to use the following copyright material is gratefully acknowledged:

Poems from *The Bloomingdale Papers* by Hayden Carruth, © 1974. Reprinted by permission of The University of Georgia Press.

Poems from *From Snow and Rock, from Chaos* by Hayden Carruth, © 1965, 1966, 1969, 1970, 1971, 1972, 1973. Reprinted by permission of New Directions Publishing Corporation.

Poems from *Brothers, I Loved You All* by Hayden Carruth, © 1978. Reprinted by permission of The Sheep Meadow Press.

CONTENTS

Hayden Carruth is a poet of unusual range and unusual depth. One of the most striking things about his work is his ability to enter the lives of other people—ordinary men and women—and tell their tales. Perhaps by virtue of his having lived many years in poverty, in the hard world, he is more able than most to sympathize and identify with people like himself. But it is a gift, really, and as one reads, one has the odd feeling that Carruth knows these people from the inside. I think this is so because he knows them through their speech. There is a reciprocity in all this, however. In telling their tales, he finds a means to express his own inner life. He gives them a voice, they give him a language.

He also writes about himself directly: his friendships with musicians, his time in a psychiatric hospital, his life in a Connecticut village, and most recently in upstate New York; but most of all, he writes of his experiences living with his wife and son, among beloved neighbors, in a little house in northern Vermont. Some of the poems are almost exalted in tone—with a spiritual dimension. Others are grim—what one could describe (if he will forgive me) as reverse mating calls. The voice comes from so very deep within him that each word tastes of his soul, as do tears of deepest grief on our cheeks. This is not, we realize, a man who sits down to "write a poem"; rather, some burden of understanding and feeling, some need to *know*, forces his poems into being. Thoreau said, "Be it life or death, what we crave is reality." So it is with Carruth. And even in hell, knowledge itself bestows a halo around the consciousness which, at moments, attains it.

I mentioned Carruth's range. Between the extremes—poems about others and poems of personal experience—lie many varieties of subject, manner, form. He violates the first principle of contemporary poetry, that is (a totally unfair characterization): "Don't think." He often refuses to "show" and instead "tells," though some of the poems are simply splendid word-lists that don't tell and don't show either. He uses his intelligence to the full, in meditations on the troubles of his own home and place, on our species, on the planet.

Speaking of words, Carruth is in love with them—all sorts, whether long, Latinate, and abstract or Anglo-Saxon and blunt. He dredges up ancient, rare, archaic words; modern, technical terms;

and most poignantly, the half-faded, cracked-wise words of country and small-town America, like *glomm*, and *bozo*. For Carruth words are graven images of things of the world, and he is their idolater and adores them.

Technically, he is a virtuoso. He writes subtle, finely tuned poems in rhyme and meter; syllabics; and in highly formalized free verse. He also writes free verse so invisibly artful that under its spell we are not in the presence of a poem, but of the world. He invents forms such as his "paragraphs" and "georgics"—the latter end-rhymes syllables within words by systematic use of hyphenation.

Carolyn Kizer once replied to someone who asked her what it takes to be a poet: "It is necessary to be absolutely shameless." Carruth is not a "confessional poet" as the term is used, but he is absolutely shameless. Whether writing of others or himself, he has only that one desire: to know all he can and to say it fully. And far from being convoluted or self-absorbed, he is at the same time one of our most clear-eyed, other-seeing, sympathizing, dependably sane observers of the actual world. More than in the case of any other poet, Carruth responds to Whitman's words: "I was the man, I suffer'd, I was there." We are lucky to have him among us.

Galway Kinnell
1985

On a Certain Engagement South of Seoul

A long time, many years, we've had these wars.
When they were opened, one can scarcely say.
We were high school students, no more than sophomores,

When Italy broke her peace on a dark day,
And that was not the beginning. The following years
Grew crowded with destruction and dismay.

When I was nineteen, once, the surprising tears
Stood in my eyes and stung me, for I saw
A soldier in a newsreel clutch his ears

To hold his face together. Those that paw
The public's bones to eat the public's heart
Said far too much, of course. The sight, so raw

And unbelievable, of people blown apart
Was enough to numb us without that bark and whine.
We grew disconsolate. Each had his chart

To mark on the kitchen wall the battle-line,
But many were out of date. The radio
Droned through the years, a faithful anodyne.

Yet the news of this slight encounter somewhere below
Seoul stirs my remembrance: we were a few,
Sprawled on the stiff grass of a small plateau,

Afraid. No one was dead. But we were new—
We did not know that probably none would die.
Slowly, then, all vision went askew.

My clothing was outlandish; earth and sky
Were metallic and horrible. We were unreal,
Strange bodies and alien minds; we could not cry

For even our eyes seemed to be made of steel;
Nor could we look at one another, for each
Was a sign of fear, and we could not conceal

Our hatred for our friends. There was no speech.
We sat alone, all of us, trying to wake
Some memory of the selves beyond our reach.

That place was conquered. The nations undertake
Another campaign now, in another land,
A stranger land perhaps. And we forsake

The miseries there that we can't understand
Just as we always have. And yet my glimpse
Of a scene on the distant field can make my hand

Tremble again. How quiet we are. One limps.
One cannot walk at all. Or one is all right.
But one owns this experience that crimps

Forgetfulness, especially at night.
Is this a bond? Does this make us brothers?
Or does it bring our hatred back? I might

Have known, but now I do not know. Others
May know. I know when I walk out-of-doors
I have a sorrow not wholly mine, but another's.

Matisse

The swift incursions of the sun
Through palms beyond the window made
This room coruscant, bayadere,
A pool where deep transversions etched
Splendors unseen from air, from air;
Fortunate attitudes in blue,
Azure in shadows which were brune,
Soft sea-like surges, lentando, poised,
All fanfares of the reeling blue
Loosed by a mote of wild cerise;
Not seen, under the old chicane
Of pose and memory, not seen
From the complacent chaise, not seen
By her, our pleasure, sitting there.
Yet now how is it we should know
These emanations, tinglings, glows,
Prismatic atoms flowing, real
And rare, out from the world of lines?
As if imagination dwelt
In the smoky sunlight, probing where
It fell—the stones, the arms and heads,
The balustrades—a moody gist
Emerged in the room's surprising hues,
But no, imagination's sun
Streamed only in the brush, Maestro,
For which the dogmas of our thanks.

Anxiety

April. Cold
Winds leach the gold
Of the sun, white
Clouds stop the light.
The torn sky rages,
And what assuages
A grief of reason
Now in this season?

April. Pale hills
And the daffodils,
Willow and brook,
Cry, "Look, look,"
Where he, the walker,
The dumb self-stalker,
Staggers, tip-toe,
Avid to know
But fearful to tread
His path of dread;
Wind, sun
Cry, "Hoo, poor one
Walking the meadow—
Where is your shadow?"

April. A tree
Cries, "I," the free
And certain swallows
Skim the hollows,
Sufficient as air
Everywhere.
The damned earth
Heaves in rebirth
In April, freeing
Anthems of being,
Atom, planet,

Petal or granite,
Identities singing
Like crazy bell-ringing.

But person is gone.
The walker steps on,
Wired by pain
To his bones, insane
In the final danger
Of loss, of anger;
He runs in the meadow
Where he casts no shadow.
And the separate wits
Of his brain are bits
Of memory falling,
Crying, and calling.
And in the cold spring
The wind is singing.

Lines Written in an Asylum

Lost sweetheart, how our memories creep
Like chidden hounds, and come to reap
All fawningly their servient due,
Their tax of pity and of rue,
So that my hope of sanity,
Like sternness, dies and falls from me.
The day I build with plotted hours
To stand apart is mine, not ours.
Its joyless business is my cure;
Stern and alone, I may endure.
But memory though it slumber wakes,
And deep in the mind its havoc makes.
The distant baying reels and swells
And floods the night, and so dispels
My hardness; hours dissolve and fall:
My loss is double: you, then all.
Dearest, are you so unaware?
For here, in mine, your senses share
These broken hours and tumbled days
That are no longer mine. Your ways,
The body's blossoms, breast and eye,
The soft leaves of your hands, the shy
And quick amusement of your smile—
My constant losses, these beguile
All my new bravery away.
If you have gone, why do you stay?
If here, then why have we no ease?
Loss is a blindness that still sees,
Loss is a ravage of the will.
A handless love that touches still.
And the incontinence of loss,
Pure loneliness, turns all to dross,
Love to a raging discontent
And self to a shabby tenement.
The mind is hapless, torn by dreams

Where all becoming only seems
A false, impossible return
To a world I labor to unlearn.

November: Indian Summer

The huge frostbank of the North
Leans over these few days.
Sunlight crumbles in haze,
Saffron of smell and color.
And the chickadees hold forth,
Thick in the ruined quince,
Scolding our complex dolor,
Talkative though long since
We came to a solemn season.
Close your eyes. The warmth
Of sun and the chickadee song
Will take you, against all reason,
To another time on the earth
That was idle and August-long,
When katydids twanged the skies
In peace, months past and more,
Far in your thoughts, as far,
Perhaps, if you close your eyes,
As the summer before the war.

Museum Piece

The eye that made this saw no pallor,
But golden and blue paint;
Now on the dry wood the color
Is tenuous and faint.

Yet under the scratches our close study
Retrieves for our curious eyes
God raising the small from the larger body,
And there the new Eve lies.

Would we smile fondly in our pride?
Ours is a long descent,
Worked in the flesh of a tiny bride
Scarce fit for ravishment,

And she, discovering she was woman,
Measured her strength of will,
By which we estimate the human
And sorrow and courage still.

But listen. Beneath the veiling scratches,
Time's ancientest filigree,
Eve in a little girl's voice beseeches
Someone to set her free.

The Sound of Snow

Snow falls in the dusk of Connecticut. The stranger
Looks up to the glutenous sky, and it is remembrance
That tickles the end of his nose like the fingertips
Of a child and remembrance that touches the end of his
Tongue with the antique purity and coolness of the snow,
As if this were almost the beginning, the first snowstorm
Fluttering between his house and the serious hemlocks.

And best of all is the sound of snow in the stillness,
A susurration, the minute percussion of settling flakes;
And the stranger listens, intent to the whispering snow
In the fir boughs, earth's most intimate confiding,
And he thinks that this is the time of sweet cognizance
As it was once when the house, graying in old dusk,
Knew him and sang to him, before the house forgot.

In the last moments of day the earth and the sky
Close in the veils of snow that flutter around him,
Shutting him in the sphere of the storm, where he stands
In his elephantine galoshes, peering this way and that
At the trees in their aloofness and the nameless house
Vanishing into the dark; and he stamps his feet urgently,
Turning as if in anger away from an evil companion.

And when, like a warning just at the fall of darkness,
Yellow light cries from the window above in the house,
From the boy's room, from the old sixteen-paned window,
The stranger remembers the boy who sits in the light
And turns the glass sphere, watching to see the snowstorm
Whirling inside. And the stranger shivers and listens
To the ceaseless unintelligible whispering of the snow.

The Birth of Venus

Surely we knew our darkling shore.
None doubted that continual roar
Of gray waves seething, cold and huge;
None misconceived that beach, those reeds
Wreathed in the dark, dead, dripping weeds.
No fiction there, no subterfuge.

Came she then, borne from such sea-bed?
We think so. Clouds in violent red
Shone on her warmly, flank and breast,
And some remember how the foam
Swirled at her ankles. Other some
Look shrewd and smile behind the rest.

She gave us beauty where our eyes
Had seen but need, and we grew wise
For wisdom could not fail the gift
Bestowed in that superb undress,
Value devised as loveliness
From ocean's riches, ocean's thrift.

But, Love, then must it be the sea
That makes you credible, must we
Bear all to one phenomenon?
Aye, certainty is our seacoast,
The landmark of the plainly lost
Whose gathering waves drive on and on.

Great queen, an ignorant poet's heart
Is all his faith, and yet his art
Can prick your source to tell the truth.
So teach him, lady. Then always
Among the voices here that praise
Your powers, one will be Carruth.

FROM The Norfolk Poems

(1962)

A Short-Run View

"In the long run aesthetics is the study of the unattain-
able, if not the unknowable. . . ."—Marcus of Pavonia

I am speaking here of beauty in all its aspects.
The town of Norfolk is situate, as lawyers say,
Interjacent to Canaan and Winsted on Rt. 44
In the high valley of the Blackberry River, tightly
Bedded in the Litchfield Hills—a lateral appendage
Of the lower Berkshires; Massachusetts lies
Four miles north. If it possessed no other
Distinction, Norfolk would be the world's creditor
Each June for its rhododendron and mountain laurel.
In fact, however, it enjoys other marks of favor.
Although the town cherishes its genteel repose,
It contains, for instance, three notable oddballs,
Brendan Gill, James Laughlin, and the undersigned.
On Bald Mountain View Road lives a cow that tilts,
Not against windmills, but against small open
Sports cars—a most Lawrentian cow. The post office
In Norfolk is the ugliest post office ever built
In the United States or dominions, but it houses
By far the best postal staff. There are a number
Of millionaires in Norfolk, which adds a good deal
To the scenery, but also a number of people who are
Content not to be millionaires, which adds even more.
Norfolk is cold in the winter; it is called
"The Ice-Box of Connecticut," and the local agent
Of the federal weather bureau has been enjoined
By the real estate interests to place his thermometer
In Ted Childs's swamp, the warmest part of town,
So as not to frighten away the prospective buyers.
One year there was frost in every month, so
I am told by Mrs. Barnes, whose family has lived
In Norfolk for generations; like other proper
Norfolkians, she pronounces it Norfork. I
Recommend to the Ritz the strawberries of
A. M. Eaton and the sweet corn sold under the sign
Of Native Fresh Vegetables on the road to Canaan.

The Smyth's retriever is named Chet, after Chet
Huntley. Mr. Hayes, proprietor of the Esso Station
On the Winsted Road, specializes in the upkeep
Of classical cars, e.g. 1925 Lincolns and 1937
Cords, but his work on all cars is of a high order.
The village green contains the most magnificently
Priapic fountain I have ever seen in America,
And also, painted on a board and tacked to an elm,
The worst poem on the subject of trees I have ever
Read; considering Kilmer, it is a feat of
Remarkable ingenuity. The library, on the other
Hand, possesses a good selection of books
And a reading room where smoking is permitted.
Astonishing! There are many foreign cars, but
Only two properly classifiable as sports cars,
My dilapidated MG and a gleaming red Triumph
That lives by the Canaan Road. In summer
The Yale School of Music and Art produces,
In addition to a certain amount of moonstaring
And handholding on the village green, music,
Excellent music, and art, not so excellent;
And on Canaan Mountain the Yale Arboretum for
The Study of Tree Genetics also produces music,
A slower and possibly even more excellent harmony.
But Ted Childs knows more about trees than anyone.
Here is a catalogue of some local placenames:
Tobey Pond, Tibbals Hill, Haystack Mountain,
Turkey Cobble, Crissey Pond, Wangum Pond, Great
Bear Swamp, Old Man McMullen Pond, Lovers Lane
(A paved street, with no apostrophe), the redundant
Pond Hill Pond, the Mad River (which washed away
A good bit of Winsted five years ago), College Hill
(Not an academy in sight), and just over the line
In Massachusetts, East Indies Pond—I don't know
Why. My favorite is Seldom Seen Pond, unknown
Except to the U. S. geological surveyors. We have
A fantastic organization called the Norfolk
Curling Club; I have not seen it in action,
But I hope they use highland whisky. Also:
Ye Olde Newgate Coon Club, the Doolittle Club,
The Country Club, and in fact more clubs than a

Self-respecting town of 2000 souls ought to allow;
To say nothing of the Norfolk Savings Bank, which is
A cavern of gloom and I suspect also the last strong-
Hold of the Lower Berkshire Anti-Jeffersonian Society.
A few other names must be included: the Hauges
And the beautiful Rose Marie, Mrs. Tyrrell,
Leon & Dorothy Deloy, Mahalia Fields, Theodore
Sylvernale (a dead shot), Wonza Hunt, the Drs.
Barstow and Blatz, Izzy Tadiello, and Joe
Pallone.* The famous residents of Norfolk—five or
Six in number—will get no additional publicity here.
I myself live in the woods near Tobey Pond; I am
A newcomer, but if Norfolkians disdain my views
As mere first impressions, let them think twice,
Lest a longer acquaintanceship should prove me wrong
Not only as a critic but as a panegyrist.

> * Addenda on proof: Nor may I neglect Leila (the
> Lovely), my friend Paul, Tanio, Annie Dixon,
> The younglings (Robert, Henry, Leon, and Bry),
> Mrs. Bellamy, Miss O'Connell, and of course
> Joanie Curtiss—but many shall go unnamed.

The Wild Swans at Norfolk

To begin with there are
No wild swans at Norfolk,
This other Norfolk
Where James Laughlin lives
With his red-haired Ann.

There are towhees and wrens
And soft yellow sapsuckers
And Blackburnian warblers
And gray owls and barred owls
And flickers but there are
No wild swans.

I can invent the swans.
They wheel on thunder's
Hundred throbbing wings
Down the sweet curve
Of Tobey Pond, pounding
The blocks of air
As trains in my childhood
Pounded their rails.

They are real wild swans;
And even though this summer
I turn forty and am deserted
By the young woman I love,
I have grown sick of emblems.
I have seen this place
On the map, and the names of
The people of Norfolk appear
On voting lists and tax rolls.

Hear how the swans converse
(As they break wing for landing)
In a rude, lightning tongue.
I cannot understand,
But clearly the swans know
What they are talking about.

Meadow House

"No house should ever be *on* any hill or on anything.
It should be *of* the hill, belonging to it, so hill and
house could live together the happier for each other."
—Frank Lloyd Wright

This is a poem for you, Ann. Impromptu,
Falling out of my precipitate brain faster
Than light dropping through a torn cloud.

And the typewriter lags. Catch up, I say!
How the wood and stone must have lagged for
Wright looking at a trance-house on a hill.

At least you and I have the advantage of not
Being architects, who fret in houses they build
And go thoroughly mad in houses they do not build.

You can live in a house. Wright wouldn't have liked
Meadow House, his style being something different,
But Meadow House lives on the hill naturally.

As naturally as the birches. And Mr. Wright
With his artist's complacency could not believe
That houses grow and very seldom are built.

(Poems too. As the light grows when it plunges
Through the torn cloud like a taproot seeking
The needed humane sustenance for heaven.)

The house grew on the hill, the woman grew
In the house, the birches grew in the meadow,
The hill is growing, I see it change every day.

No one knows why. Growing is a word
That has never been defined, not even in
My huge thirty-five-dollar dictionary.

But the end of growth, which never really ends,
Is always perfection, even if ugly or sore,
Because growth proceeds by means of balances.

(And the end of growth is always a phase
To be left behind. And real ugliness
Does not grow but arises from destruction.)

Of course Meadow House has nothing ugly;
Only balances, arrangements in which I move
Without seeming to make any displacement.

I hope there is none, because this is what
I knew many years ago and then forgot,
Forgot. It is the service of friendliness.

Ho-Hum Again

Having lost the woman I loved
    I am of course heartbroken,
In a dying summer embarked on war
When many good folk are heartsore
    And one heart is a small token.

Too small to be taken seriously.
    Death creeps in the air like pollen,
Seeding amazement in lovely eyes,
Hers too that were my enterprise
    When reason had not fallen.

Purana, Meaning Once Upon a Time

Only the gods may act with perfect impudence—
That is, irrationally. Listen while I retell
A story from a book as old as the Tobey Woods.

It fell on an autumn night, when the forest leaves
Moved like small rustling animals over the moss
And Jumna flowed with a sure deep-running strength,

That Sri Krishna played his flute by the riverbank
And the moonlight dripped like rain from tangled trees.
The music of love came liquidly to the village

Where gopis, who were the milkmaids, drank willlessly,
Their souls tipped to the song in unimagined thirst;
And soon they ran unresistingly to the forest,

One by one, and in groups, tripping and hurrying,
Leaving parents, brothers, sisters, husbands behind,
Leaving their babies whimpering in the cradles.

They said: "Ah, heavily love-laden we will give all."
Conceive the bewilderment in their eyes when Krishna,
Surrounded, the good looks of him bruising the girls,

Rebuked them, saying: "What! Have you come in the night?
Through the forest? Then you care nothing for tigers?
Shame! Respectable girls running after a lover

In the night, sacrificing your lords and your parents,
Your brothers and sisters and children. Pretty girls,
Go back to your places, go back and be content."

Tears melted their eyes and their hearts were frightened;
They looked miserably at one another in their confusion,
And began to scratch the ground with their feet like deer.

At last they said: "Truly we must attend our husbands
And our parents and children, but O Sweet Lord,
When thou art husband, parent, and child is it not just

That we seek the pleasures of all of these in Thee?"
The All-One turned away and I think said nothing,
And sorely, wearily the milkmaids returned to the village,

Their question unanswered. The singing hermit thrush
In Tobey Woods has brought this to my mind.
The leaves are beginning to fall. Soon he will be gone.

Improvisation on a Theme by Mrs. Pomeroy

Notice this strange mystique
Condemning self-pity:
We call a man weak
Or even dotty

Whom we may hear bemoaning
His long nightwatch,
And girls seem unbecoming
Who cry too much.

Christ, aren't we all such creatures
As in the soul
And flesh of our born natures
Are pitiful?

Consider the human death.
No full stop
Comes when the stifling breath
Merely gives up,

But for a certain moment
Warmth remains,
The packed cells stay animate
While the spirit drains.

In a deathly, draining world,
Though very nervous,
Thus we stay, keeping curled
To someone who'll love us.

Well, I have been forsaken,
Like some of you;
My friends, you are not mistaken,
I am pitiful too.

On Canaan Mountain Meadow

Of course, mankind—and the brain of it, brawn of it;
Enormous, as I too have marveled many a time
And will again.

But today its littleness I would moderately disparage,
That makes the stone a thing that is less than stone,
A dolmen, a god.

I say the stone is a greatness, itself in its grain,
Meaning more than a meaning, and more than a mind
May diminish.

In the sun in the field in the churchly changes of weather,
The stone lies ample and smooth and warm and brown
And at the same time blonde.

I am stroking the stone with my fingers and my curved palm,
And it is as soft as linen, and flows like the flax
From the spindle.

I would lie on the stone, reaching my arms down strongly
To draw myself full to the stone and to fondle
The flesh-gloss below.

I would copulate with the stone until I became like stone,
A slow, long spasm of love, I working calmly in love
All summer.

Naming for Love

These are the proper names:
Limestone, tufa, coral rag,
Clint, beer stone, braystone,
Porphyry, gneiss, rhyolite,
Ironstone, cairngorm, circle stone,
Blue stone, chalk, box stone,
Sarsen, magnesia, brownstone,
Flint, aventurnine,
Soapstone, alabaster, basalt,
Slate, quartzite, ashlar,
Clunch, cob, gault, grit,
Buhrstone, dolomite,
Flagstone, freestone, sandstone,
Marble, shale, gabbro, clay,
Adamant, gravel, traprock,
And of course brimstone.

Some of the names are shapes:
Crag, scarp, moraine, esker,
Alp, hogback, ledge, tor,
Cliff, boulder, crater,
Gorge, and bedrock.

Some denote uses:
Keystone, capstone,
Hearthstone, whetstone,
And gravestone.

For women a painful stone called
Wombstone, which doctors say is
"A calculus formed in the uterus."
Gallstone and kidneystone hurt everyone.
Millstone is our blessing.

I will not say the names
Of misnamed precious stones.

But a lovely name is gold,
A product of stone.

Underwards is magma;
May all who read this live long.

Adolf Eichmann

I want no tricks in speaking of this man.
My friends deplore my metaphysical mind,
But now I am a plain and plain-spoken man.

In my life only two men have turned my mind
To vengefulness, and one was this man's chief,
Who was, I now think, probably out of his mind.

But this one is rational. Naturally a mad chief
Needs sane lieutenants. Both were named Adolf,
An ugly Teutonic word which means the chief,

And earlier, in the cold north forest, this Adolf
Meant the wolf, a favorite totem. Let disgrace,
I say, fall for all time to come upon Adolf,

And let no child hereafter bear the disgrace
Of that dirty name. Sometimes in my bed
I study my feet, noticing their disgrace,

For the human foot is an ugly thing. But my bed
Is nothing like the bed that I have seen
Where hundreds of unclothed bodies lay. That bed

Was for dead people, deeply dug, and whoever has seen
Their feet knows the real ugliness and in their voice
Has heard the only true language. I have seen

And I have heard, but my feet live and my voice
Is beautiful and strong, and I say let the dung
Be heaped on that man until it chokes his voice,

Let him be made leprous so that the dung
May snuggle to his bone, let his eyes be shut
With slow blinding, let him be fed his own dung,

But let his ears never, never be shut,
And let young voices read to him, name by name,
From the rolls of all those people whom he has shut

Into the horrible beds, and let his name
Forever and ever be the word for hate,
Eichmann, cast out of the race, a loathsome name

For another kind, a sport spawned in hate
That can never be joined, never, in the world of man.
Lord, forgive me, I cannot keep down my hate.

A Leaf from Mr. Dyer's Woods

I don't know why or how
Sometimes in August a maple
Will drop a leaf burned through
Its tender parts with coral
While the veins keep green—
A rare device of color.
When I found such a one
I acted the despoiler,
Taking it from the woods
To give a friend for a trifle,
But her mind was on good deeds
And I turned shy and fearful.

Notes from Robin Hill Cottage

One small joy still left
To a writer who has grown wise
In his profession and swift
In the making of similes

Is to discover a word
He has not used before,
An ordinary one just heard
In its whole force and humor.

I think I have not written
The verb *to shed* in all
The twenty years I've given
To saving my wordy soul.

·   ·   ·

As, when I was a drunkard
And staggered to my bed,
Wholly looped and tuckered,
One by one I'd shed

My clothes upon the floor
Until at last, all naked,
I'd tumble with a snore
Into my loyal blankets,

So, when I was reformed
And stumbled onward yet,
Trembling, cold, alarmed,
Then one by one I shed

Each of my heart's desires
Like garments until I fell
Naked among these firs
And the embrace of these hills.

.   .   .

A man is like all earth's fruit,
You preserve him dry or pickled,
It's taking him in and out
That makes him come unbuckled.

.   .   .

Firtrees surround me here,
The deeper woods have ash,
Larch and oak and cedar,
The wild cherry and the beech.

Not mine; no more these walls,
The clapboard or the slate,
That house me on Robin Hill
And another man's estate.

You can't push a metaphor
And I won't speak of clothes,
But my best home so far
Is here in a borrowed house.

Older, yet I am cleanly,
Freer, yet fierce of mind,
And the mountain summer greenly
Calls winter close behind.

.   .   .

I keep a whiskey bottle
Unsealed on my kitchen shelf
For friends who come to tipple
And to tease me and to scoff.

Friends are so often blind,
Or scared to agree in public
That booze and a bullet-wound
Are one to an alcoholic.

We live alone in the cottage,
Married, the bottle and I,
Good mates going down in courage
To die independently.

      .   .   .

A bottle's a genial spouse
But in some precise respects
Does not make glad a house;
What manages that is sex.

Now I'm not vain nor choosy,
Miss Marilyn Monroe
I imagine would be a doozey,
Or La Belle Dame Bardot.

Sometimes such folk are married,
And sometimes not. Me too.
Is your husband shucked—or buried?
Drop by for an interview.

Another Catalogue

One of the commonest lunacies
That come with age is
Verbomania, and it has many
Forms, including the wild
And horrible verbigeration,
A broken mind repeating
The same words over and over
Like a broken phonograph.
I heard it many times
When I was in the asylum.

I ought to be more careful
About such things, I suppose,
But . . . *fortuna favet fatuis.*

Here is a catalogue
Of products manufactured from
Open hearth and bessemer steel:
Hot rolled billets, blooms,
Slabs, sheet bars, skelp,
Bands, flats, and hexagons,
Rounds, squares, angles, beams,
Tees, zees, and channels,
Agricultural shapes, light weight
Stair stringer channels, and
Many kinds of plates;
Railroad spikes and plates;
Bars for concrete reinforcement;
Forging steel; jalcase steel;
Cold finished rounds, squares,
Hexagons, flats, free cutting
Screw stock, pump rods, and
Shafting (turned and ground,
Turned and polished, or cold
Drawn); junior beams; piling,
Columns, girders, trusses,
Plate work, tanks, barges;
Standard pipe and line pipe,
Casing, tubing, drive and drill

Pipe (lapwelded or seamless);
Wire rods, wire (bright,
Annealed, and galvanized),
Spring wire, barbed wire,
Woven fencing and staples;
And coke tin plate and black
Sheets and other tin mill
And coke by-products.

Inevitable Didactic

The cottage is small but strongly built,
Slate, brick, and chestnut all the best,
And I curl inside like a child in a quilt,
Cozy and free in my dreams and warm,
As my poems curl, I hope, in their form,
Snugly protected but never oppressed.

R.M.D.

"There's rosemary, that's for remembrance . . ."

Somewhere in the hour
Or two or three
While I was by this flower
Meaning constancy
Seven winds cried in a tower
Hollowly.

FROM Nothing for Tigers

(1965)

The Event Itself

A curious reticence afflicts my generation, faced with the
    holocaust;
We speak seldom of the event itself, but only of what will
    be lost;
We, having betrayed our fathers and all our silent grandfathers,
    cannot cry out for ourselves, the present and tempest-tossed.

But many things and all manner of things will be hurled
In a force like dawnlight breaking, and the billion bagpipes of
    our screams will be skirled
Stupendously month after month, the greatest pain ever known
    in the world.

There will be some instantly indistinguishable from the molten
    stone;
But most will have bleeding, burning, gangrene, the sticking-out
    bone;
Men, women, and little children will be made pregnant of the
    nipping crab whose seed will be universally sown.

In the screaming and wallowing one thought will make each
    eye stare,
And that thought will be the silence pressing down at the end
    of the air,
Soon to smother the last scream forever and everywhere.

For the last man in the world, dying, will not know that he is
    the last,
But many will think it, dying; will think that in all the vast
And vacant universe they are the final consciousness, going out,
    going out, going out, with nothing to know it has passed.

The Saving Way

When the little girl was told that the sun someday,
In a billion years or a trillion, will burn out dead,
She sobbed in a fierce and ancient way
And stamped and shook her head

Till the brown curls flew; and I wondered how,
Given the world, given her place and time,
She should ever come in her own right mind to know
That it all may happen one day before her prime,

The lights go out in one crude burst
Or slowly, winking across the cold,
The last and worst
That the old time's craziest prophet had foretold;

And I wondered also how she shall come to find
The town whose monuments
Are the rusty barbed wire rattling in the wind
And the shredding tents

And the street where the bodies crawl
Forever and ever, our broken dead
Who arise again, and again and always fall
For a word that someone said;

Or how she shall seek the plundered isles
Adrift on the smoking seas,
Or the desert bloodied for miles and miles,
Or the privacies

Of Jews laid out in a snowy woods,
Black men laid in the swamp,
All in their sorrowing attitudes
Of inquiry; or how when the wind is damp

She shall come someday to the marble square
Where papers blow and her father stands
In idle discourse with a millionaire
Who will rape her later on with his own hands;

And I wondered finally how all this
Will be anything to secure
What she knows now in her child's instinct is
The sole world, immensely precious and impure.

My dear, will you learn the saving way?
And then can we go,
In keen joy like Lear and like Cordelia gay,
To invent our lives from these great days of woe?

Burning Dawn

This day lies under glass,
A relic. Blear and wan,
Two feet wade up the dawn,
Tread and fall back like fish,
Two fish as blind as bone.
The sun, the sun beats down.
A vitreous, brittle sky
Expands to the breaking point
Like burnt glass being blown,
And the blind feet go on.
Nothing can keep it now,
This sky that splits apart,
For the cygnet and the swan
On striding wings have flown
Over the shallow hill,
Dripping across the lawn
Droplets of breaking laughter
Like that of the soulless girl
Who was here and has gone.

Ontological Episode of the Asylum

The boobyhatch's bars, the guards, the nurses,
The illimitable locks and keys are all arranged
To thwart the hand that continually rehearses
Its ending stroke and raise a barricade
Against destruction-seeking resolution.
Many of us in there would have given all
(But we had nothing) for one small razor blade
Or seventy grains of the comforting amytal.

So I went down in the attitude of prayer,
Yes, to my knees on the cold floor of my cell,
Humped in a corner, a bird with a broken wing,
And asked and asked as fervently and well
As I could guess to do for light in the mists
Of death, until I learned God doesn't care.
Not only that, he doesn't care at all,
One way or the other. That is why he exists.

Existence Before Essence

We rolled apart on the forest floor
(Remember?), each in a sighing terror,
As Hector after one battle more,
Sighing, turned to the armor-bearer
With his black lance in that black war.

Darling, then as the leaves plunged down
I knew the peril of such deep giving
(Leaves of aspen, leaves of rowan)
And the uselessness of such retrieving
Under a woods gone all nut-brown.

Thalassa

In passion I bent to the march, treading, treading,
Comrade to all but most to obedient women,
Yet hung on their last resistance, so degrading
A treadmill, hung on the speck of the superhuman
In passion's depths denying my urgent reading
As if it were an impenetrable omen
In the bowels of love, or as if I were parading
Falsely among them, the pimpliest catechumen,

Until my sickness came and I lay still.
Abandoned then in that country for a long, long time,
One day I heard in my head like a distant bell
The sound *Thalassa!* And as the hawk will climb
In an empty sky, look down, and plunge at will,
I saw to their naked hearts, the foul, the sublime.

Godhulivela

The poets of the Land of Indra write
Godhulivela, end of day, "the hour
The cows make dusty," and a lotus flower
In my eyes lays its petals to the light

Of August evenings. Simply, this is how
The word in darkness lain two thousand years
And experience lost for thirty, hemispheres
Falling each way divisive of the two—

As we say, worlds apart—at last may join,
Something won back from chaos though by chance,
Godhulivela. The muddy cows advance,
Flicking their tails, Sad Udder, Bony Loin,

And Rolling Eye following one by one
Around the knoll, the duckpond, past the stile,
My lumbering, lowing, suffering, lingering file.
The saffron dust of evening cloaks the sun.

The poets of the Land of Tophet know
The word, could write it if they were inclined
To call that fading resonance to mind;
Their children would not understand them though.

The poets of the Land of Indra may
Consider this a mute and frightening end,
Something far too remote to comprehend,
But doubtless it will come to them someday.

The Smallish Son

A small voice is fretting my house in the night,
a small heart is there . . .
                              Listen,
I who have dwelt at the root of a scream forever,
I who have read my heart like a man with no hands
reading a book whose pages turn in the wind,
I say listen, listen, hear me
in our dreamless dark, my dear. I can teach you complaining.
My father, being wise, knowing the best rebellion is at forty,
told me to wait; but when he was sixty
he had nothing to say. Then do not wait.
Could I too not tell you much of a young man's folly?
But you will learn. When you play at strife-of-the-eyes
with existence, staring at the fluorescent moon to see
which of you will go under, please, please
be the first to smile. Do not harden yourself
though it means surrendering all, turning yourself out
to be known at the world's mercy. You will lose your name,
you will not know the curious shape of your coat,
even the words you breathe, spoken out so clearly,
will loosen and disperse forever, all given over
to the wind crying upon distant seas. Moment of horror:
the moonlight will name you, a profile among fallen flowers.
Yet you may survive, for many have done so. You need
only to close your eyes, beautiful feminine gesture;
and do not be afraid of the strange woman you find
lying in the chamber of your throat. When a silver bird
strikes at the shutters of your eyes with his wings
admit him, do not attempt to tame him, but as he swoops
in the tall glimmer of your intricate room
admire his freedom; and when a silver mouse
scurries twittering through the passageways of your blood
consider his beauty. So it will be: dark, a long vigil,
far among splendors of despair, this creation
in the closed eye. Everything will be true, pure,
your love most of all, and your flesh in the drunkenness
of becoming a dream. Lingering among the revenants
who still bear your name, touching and kissing,

dancing among their tatters of skin and splintered bones,
noticing the song of the tomb, how it soars in dream,
you in your sovereignty condescending to song,
permitting your myth—what awareness then, what ecstasies
in the shimmering dark pool, what marvels of the dark stair!
But now, please open your eyes again. Have we not said
down with all tyrants, even our own? Especially our own!
Open your eyes; they will glitter from long sleep
with the knowledge of the other side of the world.
Their light then will be of such a quiet intensity
that smiles and frowns will fall away like shadows
of wild birds flying over. No complicity, no acquiescence;
and yet a degree of affection remaining, as when one finds
an old bible in an old cupboard of an empty house.
So it is, so, freedom and beauty. Do not be modest,
wear the delicate beauty of those crippled at birth
who earn the grace of their maiming. Do not be afraid,
assume the freedom of those born in their captivity
who earn the purity of their being. All one and all many,
but remember, never the two alone, falsely dividing
in the mind's paralyzed divorce. This is our meaning
under our true rebellion, this is the dark where we
may venture without our dreams. In the dreamless dark
where I await you, the dark light of my eyes
may still be darkly burning when you come.
You must look and you must seek
for my eyes will answer but I think they will not summon.
And if you do not find them, turn away.

Freedom and Discipline

Saint Harmony, many
years I have stript

naked in your service
under the lash. Yes,

I believe the first
I heard (living, there

aloud in the hall) was
Sergei Rachmaninoff

set at the keys like a
great dwarf, a barrel

on three spindles,
megalocephalus, hands

with fourteen fingers,
ugly as Merlin, with whom

I was in love, a boy and
an old man; a boy nodding

and an old man sorrowing
under the bushfire of the

people's heart, until he
coolly knocked out the

Prelude in C♯ Minor. Second
was Coleman Hawkins

in about 1933 perhaps.
I, stript and bleeding,

leapt to the new touch,
up and over the diminished

in a full-voiced authority
of blue-gold blues. I

would do nothing, locked
in discipline, sworn to

freedom. The years shrieked
and smothered, like billboards

beside a road at night.
I learnt how Catlett

drove the beat without
harming it, how Young

sped between the notes,
how Monk reconstructed

a broken chord to make
my knuckles rattle, and much

from oblivion: Newton,
Fasola, Berigan, my

inconsolable Papa Yancey.
Why I went to verse-making

is unknowable, this
grubbing art. Trying,

Harmony, to fix your beat
in things that have none

and want none—absurdity!
Let that be the answer

to any hope of statecraft.
As Yeats said, *Fal de rol.*

Freedom and discipline concur
only in ecstasy, all else

is shoveling out the muck.
Give me my old hot horn.

(1970)

Roads wear out slowly,
but they wear out. The milestones
twinkle in long grass.

.   .   .

Fathers die, but sons
catch the grave chill, looking in
at lost forgiveness.

.   .   .

Of course they prefer
hell to loneliness, of course
they go home to die.

.   .   .

For your love given
ask no return, none. To love
you must love to love.

.   .   .

Lover to lover
gasping *now*, and a star falls,
brightens, disappears.

.   .   .

Therefore to us, time's
final lesson: be content
with no monument.

.   .   .

Reaching again, spurned
again. Cat, you fill my hand
with masochism.

.   .   .

True, I happen. So
put "I" in. But randomly,
I am not the song.

.   .   .

Hear the night bellow,
our great black bull. Hear the dawn
distantly lowing.

.   .   .

Niobe, your tears
are your children now. See how
we have multiplied.

        .   .   .

Let my snow-tracks lead
on, on. Let them, where they stop,
stop. There, in mid-field.

FROM From Snow and Rock,

from Chaos (1973)

Dedication in These Days

What words can make
seems next to nothing now
a tune   a measure

Yet
I have seen you with your eyes wet
with pleasure
for their sake

For this then
these few
for now   for you
again

If It Were Not for You

Liebe, meine liebe, I had not hoped
to be so poor

         The night winds reach
like the blind breath of the world
in a rhythm without mind, gusting and beating
as if to destroy us, battering our poverty
and all the land's flat and cold and dark
under iron snow

         the dog leaps in the wind
barking, maddened with winter, and his voice
claps again and again down the valley
like tatters of revolutionary pennants

                birches
cry and hemlocks by the brook
stand hunched and downcast with their hands
in their pockets

Liebe, the world is wild
and without intention

                    how far
this might be from the night of christmas
if it were not for you.

Down the reaching wind
shrieks of starlight bear broken messages
among mountains where shadows plunge
                                    yet our brightness
is unwavering
                Kennst du das land
wo die zitronen blühn, im dunkeln laub
die goldorangen . . .   liebe
art thou singing

It is a question partly
of the tree with our stars and partly
of your radiance brought from the land
where legends flower to this land
but more than these our bright poverty
is a house in the wind and a light
on the mountain

Liebe, our light rekindled
in this remoteness from the other land,
in this dark of the blue mountain where only
the winds gather
        is what we are for the time that we are
        what we know for the time that we know

How gravely and sweetly the poor touch in the dark.

Tabula Rasa

There, an evening star, there again. Above
The torn lovelace of snow, in the far sky
That glows with an afterlight, fading,

The evening star piercing a black tangle
Of trees on the ridge. Shall it be our kiss?
Can we call its sudden singleness,

Its unannounced simplicity, its rage
In the abhorrent distances, its small viridine,
Ours, always ours? Or shall we say

This wintry eloquence is mere affect
Of tattered snow, of tangling black limbs?
Everything reproaches me, everything,

Because we do not stand by Leman's water,
By the onyx columns, entablatures, all
The entablatures, watching the cygnets fade

With Sapphic pathos into a silver night.
Listen, the oboe and the little drum
Make Lulliana where the old whores walk . . .

Do men and women meet and love forthwith?
Or do they think about it? Or do they
In a masque play fated figures *en tragique?*

Perhaps they are those who only stand
In tattered snow and dream of fated things.
The limbs have snatched the star, have eaten it.

Another night, we've lost another day. Nothing
Spoke to us, certainly nothing spoke for us—
The slate is clean. Here therefore is my kiss.

Concerning Necessity

It's quite true we live
in a kind of rural twilight
most of the time giving
our love to the hard dirt
the water and the weeds
and the difficult woods

ho we say drive the wedge
heave the axe run the hand shovel
dig the potato patch
dig ashes dig gravel
tickle the dyspeptic chain saw
make him snarl once more

while the henhouse needs cleaning
the fruitless corn to be cut
and the house is falling to pieces
the car coming apart
the boy sitting and complaining
about something everything anything

this was the world foreknown
though I had thought somehow
probably in the delusion
of that idiot thoreau
that necessity could be saved
by the facts we actually have

like our extreme white birch
clasped in the hemlock's arms
or our baybreasted nuthatch
or our mountain and our stars
and really these things do serve
a little though not enough

what saves the undoubted collapse
of the driven day and the year
is my coming all at once
when she is done in or footsore
or down asleep in the field
or telling a song to a child

coming and seeing her move
in some particular way
that makes me to fall in love
all over with human beauty
the beauty I can't believe
right here where I live.

The Ravine

Stones, brown tufted grass, but no water,
it is dry to the bottom. A seedy eye
of orange hawkweed blinks in sunlight
stupidly, a mink bumbles away,
a ringnecked snake among stones lifts its head
like a spark, a dead young woodcock—
long dead, the mink will not touch it—
sprawls in the hatchment of its soft plumage
and clutches emptiness with drawn talons.
This is the ravine today. But in spring it
cascaded, in winter it filled with snow
until it lay hidden completely. In time,
geologic time, it will melt away
or deepen beyond recognition, a huge
gorge. These are what I remember and foresee.
These are what I see here every day,
not things but relationships of things,
quick changes and slow. These are my sorrow,
for unlike my bright admonitory friends
I see relationships, I do not see things.
These, such as they are, every day, every
unique day, the first in time and the last,
are my thoughts, the sequences of my mind.
I wonder what they mean. Every day,
day after day, I wonder what they mean.

Once More

Once more by the brook the alder leaves
turn mauve, bronze, violet, beautiful
after the green of crude summer; galled
black stems, pithy, tangled, twist in the
flesh-colored vines of wild cyclamen.
Mist drifts below the mountaintop
in prismatic tatters. The brook is full,
spilling down heavily, loudly, in silver
spate from the beaver ponds in the high
marshy meadows. The year is sinking:
heavily, loudly, beautifully. Deer move
heavily in the brush like bears, half drunk
on masty acorns and rotten wild apples.
The pileated woodpecker thumps a dead elm
slowly, irregularly, meditatively.
Like a broken telephone a cricket rings
without assertion in dead asters and
goldenrod; asters gone cloudy with seed,
goldenrod burnt and blackened. A gray trout
rests under the lip of glacial stone. One
by one the alder leaves plunge down to earth,
veering, and lie there, glowing, like a shirt
of Nessus. My heart in my ribs does what it
has done occasionally all my life: thumps and
heaves suddenly in irregular rhythm that makes
me gasp. How many times has this season turned
and gone down? How many! I move heavily
into the bracken, and the deer stand still
a moment, uncertain, before they break away,
snorting and bounding heavily before me.

The Cows at Night

The moon was like a full cup tonight,
too heavy, and sank in the mist
soon after dark, leaving for light

faint stars and the silver leaves
of milkweed beside the road,
gleaming before my car.

Yet I like driving at night
in summer and in Vermont:
the brown road through the mist

of mountain-dark, among farms
so quiet, and the roadside willows
opening out where I saw

the cows. Always a shock
to remember them there, those
great breathings close in the dark.

I stopped, taking my flashlight
to the pasture fence. They turned
to me where they lay, sad

and beautiful faces in the dark,
and I counted them—forty
near and far in the pasture,

turning to me, sad and beautiful
like girls very long ago
who were innocent, and sad

because they were innocent,
and beautiful because they were
sad. I switched off my light.

But I did not want to go,
not yet, nor knew what to do
if I should stay, for how

in that great darkness could I explain
anything, anything at all.
I stood by the fence. And then

very gently it began to rain.

I Know, I Remember, But How Can I Help You

The northern lights.   I wouldn't have noticed them
    if the deer hadn't told me
     a doe   her coat of pearls   her glowing hoofs
        proud and inquisitive
        eager for my appraisal
and I went out into the night with electrical steps
    but with my head held also proud
        to share the animal's fear
        and see what I had seen before
    a sky flaring and spectral
        greenish waves and ribbons
and the snow   under strange light   tossing in the pasture
    like a storming ocean caught
        by a flaring beacon.

The deer stands away from me   not far
        there among bare black apple trees
        a presence I no longer see.
We are proud to be afraid
        proud to share
the silent magnetic storm that destroys the stars
        and flickers around our heads
    like the saints' cold spiritual agonies
        of old.
I remember   but without the sense   other light-storms
    cold memories discursive and philosophical
        in my mind's burden
    and the deer remembers nothing.
We move our feet   crunching bitter snow   while the storm
    crashes like god-wars down the east
        we shake the sparks from our eyes
    we quiver inside our shocked fur
        we search for each other
    in the apple thicket—
        a glimpse, an acknowledgment
    it is enough and never enough—
we toss our heads   and say good night
    moving away on bitter bitter snow.

Emergency Haying

Coming home with the last load I ride standing
on the wagon tongue, behind the tractor
in hot exhaust, lank with sweat,

my arms strung
awkwardly along the hayrack, cruciform.
Almost 500 bales we've put up

this afternoon, Marshall and I.
And of course I think of another who hung
like this on another cross. My hands are torn

by baling twine, not nails, and my side is pierced
by my ulcer, not a lance. The acid in my throat
is only hayseed. Yet exhaustion and the way

my body hangs from twisted shoulders, suspended
on two points of pain in the rising
monoxide, recall that greater suffering.

Well, I change grip and the image
fades. It's been an unlucky summer. Heavy rains
brought on the grass tremendously, a monster crop,

but wet, always wet. Haying was long delayed.
Now is our last chance to bring in
the winter's feed, and Marshall needs help.

We mow, rake, bale, and draw the bales
to the barn, these late, half-green,
improperly cured bales; some weigh 100 pounds

or more, yet must be lugged by the twine
across the field, tossed on the load, and then
at the barn unloaded on the conveyor

and distributed in the loft. I help—
I, the desk-servant, word-worker—
and hold up my end pretty well too; but God,

the close of day, how I fall down then. My hands
are sore, they flinch when I light my pipe.
I think of those who have done slave labor,

less able and less well prepared than I.
Rose Marie in the rye fields of Saxony,
her father in the camps of Moldavia

and the Crimea, all clerks and housekeepers
herded to the gaunt fields of torture. Hands
too bloodied cannot bear

even the touch of air, even
the touch of love. I have a friend
whose grandmother cut cane with a machete

and cut and cut, until one day
she snicked her hand off and took it
and threw it grandly at the sky. Now

in September our New England mountains
under a clear sky for which we're thankful at last
begin to glow, maples, beeches, birches

in their first color. I look
beyond our famous hayfields to our famous hills,
to the notch where the sunset is beginning,

then in the other direction, eastward,
where a full new-risen moon like a pale
medallion hangs in a lavender cloud

beyond the barn. My eyes
sting with sweat and loveliness. And who
is the Christ now, who

if not I? It must be so. My strength
is legion. And I stand up high
on the wagon tongue in my whole bones to say

woe to you, watch out
you sons of bitches who would drive men and women
to the fields where they can only die.

Twilight Comes
(after Wang Wei)

Twilight comes to the little farm
At winter's end. The snowbanks
High as the eaves, which melted
And became pitted during the day,
Are freezing again, and crunch
Under the dog's foot. The mountains
From their place behind our shoulders
Lean close a moment, as if for a
Final inspection, but with kindness,
A benediction as the darkness
Falls. It is my fiftieth year. Stars
Come out, one by one with a softer
Brightness, like the first flowers
Of spring. I hear the brook stirring,
Trying its music beneath the ice.
I hear—almost, I am not certain—
Remote tinklings; perhaps sheepbells
On the green side of a juniper hill
Or wineglasses on a summer night.
But no. My wife is at her work,
There behind yellow windows. Supper
Will be soon. I crunch the icy snow
And tilt my head to study the last
Silvery light of the western sky
In the pine boughs. I smile. Then
I smile again, just because I can.
I am not an old man. Not yet.

Abandoned Ranch, Big Bend

Three people come where no people belong any more.
They are a woman who would be young
And good-looking if these now seemed
Real qualities, a child with yellow hair, a man
Hardened in desperate humanity. But here are only
Dry cistern, adobe flaking, a lizard. And now this
Disagreeable feeling that they were summoned. Sun
On the corrugated roof is a horse treading,
A horse with wide wings and heavy hoofs. The lizard
Is splayed head down on the wall, pulsing. They do not
Bother to lift their binoculars to the shimmering distance.
From this dead center the desert spirals away,
Traveling outward and inward, pulsing. Summoned
From half across the world, from snow and rock,
From chaos, they arrived a moment ago, they thought,
In perfect fortuity. There is a presence emerging here in
Sun dance and clicking metal, where the lizard blinks
With eyes whetted for extinction; then swirling
Outward again, outward and upward through the sky's
White-hot funnel. Again and again among the dry
Wailing voices of displaced Yankee ghosts
This ranch is abandoned to terror and the sublime.
The man turns to the woman and child. He has never
Said what he meant. They give him
The steady cool mercy of their unreproachful eyes.

(1974)

Eternal City

Day turning to night
without flare, end of day
and first of night
held between
one air and another air,
a significance of light
in which a figure leans
against a pillar, weeping
under a great roof
in the midst of the city,
a figure that wears
a flat-crowned, flat-brimmed
hat tilted down
such as women have worn
in some times and places.
This is a man, weeping.
His hand, heavily veined,
falls beside veined stone.
Is he weeping? His face,
withheld, hidden beneath
the tilted hat-brim,
nevertheless is the center
of the city, the cathedral,
the web of evening mist.
He is weeping. Everything
we know, that turned our steps
this way, through these old
twilit streets, past these
gardens and courtyards,
affirms his weeping.

Green Mountain Idyl

Honey   I'd split your kindling
     clean & bright
& fine
     if you was mine

baby baby
     I'd taken to you like my silky hen
my bluetick bitch my sooey sow
     my chipmunk   my finchbird
& my woodmouse
     if you was living at my house

I'd mulch your strawberries & cultivate
     your potato patch
all summer long
     & then in winter
come thirty below and the steel-busting weather
     I'd tune your distributor & adjust
your carburetor
     if me & you was together

be it sunshine be it gloom
     summer or the mean mud season
honey I'd kiss you
     every morningtime
& evenings I'd hurry
     to get shut of the barn chores early
& then in the dark of the night
     I'd stand at the top of the stairs & hold the light
for you for you
     if you'd sleep in my room

& when old crazy come down the mountain after you
     with his big white pecker in his hand
you would only holler
     & from the sugarhouse
the mow   the stable
     or wherever I'm at
I'd come   god I'd come running to you
     like a turpentined cat

64

only in our bed
    honey
no hurting
    but like as if it was
git-music
    or new-baked bread
I'd fuck so easy
    sweet-talking & full of love
if you was just my daisy
    & my dove

Rhopaloceral

When these two butterflies flutter upward toward the blue-white
agatine sky, defining in their dance of sex the loose twining rope
that gleams with vacancy in the sun, my eyes frankly sink back and
cannot climb with them: back to this end of the rope where the noose
coils, dangles, calls.

Peculiar glitter, as of something false, associated with all symmetry.
These two perfectly inversive wings; so bright, so fair to see. And
those figures there, man and man, a face intent upon the surface of
the pool.

Once a white butterfly made mirror-dancing with a white duck feather
floating down the brook. Did I imagine that?

Two small azure butterflies dancing in a pool of dust by the road;
from hill to opposing hill two chainsaws dissenting.

Wide blue sky. How many hundreds of centuries have men thought
    this
the mirror of earth, as if our niggling particularities could be so
smoothed and fused, instead of the mirror of what lies under
the earth? We on the surface are in between, caught in a mighty
reverberation of nothingness, shaken. Superficies. Powerless to deflect
the organ tone that riddles us.

These are strange butterflies, brown and blue with spots of ivory;
strangeness attracting special notice. Why not? I look into their
symmetry as into a huge dim hall hung with tapestries on either side.
I see that my imagination is the mirror of what lies there, out there;
a mirror put into me like a foreign object. My being suffers ana-
phylaxis and tries to expel the irritant, but without success. It is
I who am alien, I who am excluded. Symmetry is the sign of irrelation
and death.

The function of self-consciousness is to carry, I mean literally to
transport, these butterflies of the nonself. Can one think of
any other? It is enslavement, granted. Why am I unconsoled to hear
     that
my burden is only a butterfly?

When I thought to escape them they danced just outside the open
window high over the city street, or rested opening and closing
on the windowsill. When I hoped to join them they teased my
     clutching
eyes across the country meadow, through the umbrageous woods.

Where am I? Not locus, but substantiation; not wherein nor whereon,
but whereof. The crystal of windowpane contains, transports, trans-
mits. I am "in" the lens of my eye. I am the veriest point of
passage and reverberation.

O blue-brown-ivory twining upward into the wide sky, how marvelous
that you sustain my dead weight hanging here!

Maybe Political
(for Deianira with love)

the shirt of fire has been cast down
but gouts of flame still puff like flowers
on crisp swollen flesh   napalm down
the knoll a smear of flowers   don't
for chrissakes *doan tip it*   we eased
the 40 gallon pot of boiling fat down
from the range where the iron fireman wheezed
across a sweaty floor out a door down
oh almost down the steps   *watch it*
smoking flowers bubbling in pig fat   what shit
said charley farley   gouts of leaves
left on the maples like flowers like little
whale oil lamps in the forest down
gloomy ways   smell of diesel   lights
for dead pumpkins   the shirt lies on the ground
annually and the flesh hurts   bones
the bare bones of winter coming   burning
hurting flesh in autumnal mass under
the smoke-film where greasy joan doth
keel the pot and the brook limps
from its hole in the ground   greasy brook
limping to the sea from stone to stone
annually eternally   maybe   the worldflesh
being everything   but not measure   mark
the time-distance on this imaginary line
where cities spread from points   benchmarks
set in stone brass numbers under smoking
light   stone metal mark number   reality
doth keel the potted joan mixing things
with thoughts fires with desires   who'd dare
end war tonight for end of pain is end
and end of perishing is more same   shirt
tattered and torn melting into the ground
who can look   oh turn these eyes around

Introspectional

of the shadow cast by earth in the sun's light
way way way far away away across
the void

and of the shadow cast by earth in the light
of a far faint opposing star, cast
like a pin   in
the depths of the sun

rise & turn & sit down & raise my head
& smile   and the dog
raises his head

& howls

The Bloomingdale Papers

(1975)

Excerpts

· · ·

I know there is a country where we go
Only adventuresomely, where the bears
With summer in their bellies sink to sleep,
Abatement, a subsidence of the will
Into warm lures and ardors of their dreams.
And here the wind veers to the cold northeast.
Another oak leaf makes a silent parting
And circles downward like a swinging gull
To the sea below. And everywhere this is
The time for shoulder-turning carelessly
After a pondering glance, the withdrawing time,
Time for the turning in and inward, time
For the long, long scrutabilities of the fire.
So rich and fearful are the dreams of winter
We never mourn the filmy world outside,
We even turn our anger from the door
That opens only for someone else's key
And from the windows and their iron bars.
Prison grows warm and *is* the real asylum.
And all the terrors of our inward journeys,
The grave indecencies, the loathsome birds,
Are goads to the strange bravery we muster,
We crippled, unbrave ones; and our hard days
Become as perilous as our quilted nights.
Into quiescence we pursue our killers;
Into fell lassitude we fight our way.
And never in our drowsy eyes appears
For an instant any boredom but the sharp
Unwearying tedium of this great despair.
These are the fascinations of our winter.

· · ·

The year fell slowly.
The tilting planet sloped on its northward gyre
Languidly. Warm days lingered.
Indian summer was an endless converse
Among bored minds. I took the sun,
Its fierceness gone, trying its warmth
As old men test their baths,
And found it good. To bake one's bones
Is to ease the mysterious nerves.
On October afternoons, the morning fury over,
I lay on the lovely grass; the *plats*
Of tennis sounded distantly; crows cawed.
These were the hours of surcease, remembrances.
Sorrow and melancholy were a balm,
And I wrote a sonnet—

    Of all disquiets sorrow is most serene.
    Its intervals of soft humility
    Are lenient; they intrude on our obscene
    Debasements and our fury like a plea
    For wisdom—guilt is always shared. The fears
    Fall, if for just an hour, all away,
    And the old essential person reappears.
    Sorrow can shape us better than dismay.

    You have forgiven me, old friends and lovers,
    I think you have forgiven me at last,
    As you put by the banished fugitive.
    And if I'm sorry who was once aghast
    For all the hurts I've done you, I forgive,
    I too, the self this sorrow still recovers.

        ·   ·   ·

Ancient Mr. Barnes on Hall Five
possesses a body whose withness
                in the Whiteheadian sense
surpasses all expectations
and certainly surpasses the
                endurance of his mind.
Hence he is much jollity for the attendants.
But this morning:
      ATT. Hello, hello, Mr. Barnes. And who is
           president this morning?
      MR. B. Eisenhower, you goddamned fool!
'Sdeath!
      MR. B. And who's crazy now?
For once then not Mr. Barnes.
On another occasion
ancient Mr. Barnes
             formerly a scholar
             and I think a minister
was being conducted to the can
             when he was overcome
             by confusion.
     MR. B. Stop, stop, young man. What *is* it
       you want of me?

ATT. I want you to use the toilet, Mr. Barnes.
MR. B. What? What?
ATT. I want you to take a shit, Mr. Barnes.
MR. B. I shan't. I shan't shit.
Who's crazy now
             .   .   .

I have done a small survey, like any good Frobenius, on the present inhabitants of Hall Six.

We are 24 inmates all told.

The oldest is 76 years of age, the youngest is 19.

The one who has served the longest time in the hatch has been here thirteen years. The shortest is six weeks.

Four are repeaters; that is, this is their second sentence in this hatch. Three others were previously in other hatches.

Sixteen have had electroshock therapy.

Twelve are from New York; five from New Jersey, two from Connecticut, and one each from Kentucky, Texas, New Mexico, Alabama and England.

There are two Catholics, six Jews, ten Protestants, and five agnostics.

Unanimity of belief exists on only one proposition: man's chief joy is fornication.

The 24 inmates may be classified as follows:

> 1 accountant
> 2 salesmen
> 1 musician
> 3 businessmen (grocer, hotelkeeper, corporation executive)
> 1 priest
> 1 advertising copywriter
> 1 merchant marine
> 5 college students
> 1 playboy
> 4 doctors
> 1 taxi driver
> 1 airplane mechanic
> 1 gambler
> 1 radio announcer

They may be further classified as follows:

7 manic-depressive psychoses
(2 manic types, 3 depressive, 2 circular)
7 schizophrenia (1 simple, 1 catatonic, 5 paranoid)
1 psychasthenia
2 anxiety psychoneuroses
6 alcoholics
1 drug addict

Note: most inmates believe the alcoholics have the easiest portion; neither their illness nor their treatment seems particularly uncomfortable, even though the percentage of permanent cures is low—a little sodium amytal and some vitamin shots during the first days in the hatch are usually enough to straighten them out. The alcoholics themselves believe this and hold themselves somewhat aloof from the rest of us, who are crazy.

.   .   .

Save me, O God; for the waters are come in
          unto my soul.

I sink in deep mire, where there is no standing:
I am come into deep waters, where the floods
          overflow me.

I am weary of my crying: my throat is dried:
          mine eyes fail . . .

Deliver me out of the mire, and let me not sink:
let me be delivered from them that hate me,
          and out of the deep waters.

Let not the waterflood overflow me, neither
          let the deep swallow me up,
          and let not the pit
          shut her mouth upon me.

.   .   .

Once on a night in spring
     I remember
I sat at the end of the long curving jetty
whose base is attached to the city of Chicago—
that is to say, it bends into Lake Michigan
    from North Avenue.
I had turned my back to the city
    and I watched the stars.
It was a night to think of poems to write.
Then, weary of poems, I sprawled back
letting my head hang upsidedown from the pier.
I looked toward Chicago; the lake was above me.
In the watery sky the city shone and glimmered.
Up, up it reached, tower on tower, into
    the black depths
where fishes with alien intelligence kept
    motionless company.
And earth below me was strewn with stars.
Oh it was a dancing delicate rippling world,
  so bright, gaiety beyond noise and laughter,
in the water of all souls' drowning.
Deeply it rose, darkly it shone, and I drew
breaths of cool water, coming alive in that world.
But, magnificently, a fish jumped, and the city
flew apart, sparks in the wind,
    and only the stars were still.

       . . .

       A perfect stone
Of goodliness weighs in my mind, weathering
All the erosions that cut and wash away the soft
Groves of nerves, the silts of idleness and accident
And a thousand and one mornings. I carry it,
A treasure, everywhere, my balancing stone, my precious stone.
It is a smooth and intricate design, shaped
To a living girl, yet changeless and worn hard
By the watery or sandy winds that circulate
Through my veins. It curls inside my skull, an embrace
Close to the bone, enclosing deathlessly in stone

The only faithfulness that has endured, uninjured.
Such a companion did I pray for when I began
My journeying on the burned plain, my crouching
In the wider crater that has become my home.
And when it was given to me, a rude gift to hurt me,
I was not hurt, but thankful and pleased to possess something.
I worked with my shaping hands, molding and caressing,
To make a beautiful stone, and it has grown ever
More in grace and love, my image, my stone, my girl
Who makes me and shapes me as I turn her form
In my hands; I am the partner of the stone.
The gift that came to me from the heaven of disdain
Is my saint, my protectress, the only faith I have kept
When all the other images shattered on their screen
Like broken shadows and disintegrated in the smoke.
My monument I rescued from that other country
And brought to the burned plain, the eyeless crater.
When the fiery sun danced on the horizon, twirling
And bending in seductive sensuous gleams, I ran
Often, calling, imploring for such golden loves and truths,
But always fell, face in the sharp grass, weeping,
Until the comfort of my stone restored me, saying,
"To be true." I knew, I knew. Dancing suns
All come to this. My true stone, I was true to you,
Though I broke all the others. And one day, far
On the burned plain, the clouds in the fierce sky
Flew, and their shadows on the plain flew, and I turned fast
To find my way, but confused voices betrayed me,
Far on the burned plain. I ran that way, that way, that way,
Like three men. And the sudden dark descended with a crash.
I awoke here, with my true stone, in this graveyard
Where other journeyers have come too, bringing their stones.
Many stones are here, all true, all old and beautiful.
The savage methodical men
                    go among them with heavy hammers.
                    .   .   .

Envoi

The sun returns perforce,
Time's lenient measure thaws
Our wintry element.
For time is a long divorce
And a long, long quest for cause
That leads us to content.

FROM Brothers, I Loved

You All (1978)

The Loon on Forrester's Pond

Summer wilderness, a blue light
twinkling in trees and water, but even
wilderness is deprived now. "What's that?
What is that sound?" Then it came to me,
this insane song, wavering music
like the cry of the genie inside the lamp,
it came from inside the long wilderness
of my life, a loon's song, and there he was
swimming on the pond, guarding
his mate's nest by the shore,
diving and staying under
unbelievable minutes and coming up
where no one was looking. My friend
told how once in his boyhood
he had seen a loon swimming beneath his boat,
a shape dark and powerful
down in that silent world, and how
it had ejected a plume of white excrement
curving behind. "It was beautiful,"
he said.

The loon
broke the stillness over the water
again and again,
broke the wilderness
with his song, truly
a vestige, the laugh that transcends
first all mirth
and then all sorrow
and finally all knowledge, dying
into the gentlest quavering timeless
woe. It seemed
the real and only sanity to me.

That I Had Had Courage When Young

Yet had I not much
who went out—out!—among those
heartless all around, to look
and talk sometimes and touch?

In the big lunatic house
I did not fly apart nor spatter
the walls with myself, not quite.
I sat with madness in my mouth.

But never, it was never enough.
Else how could all these books
I did not write bend down my back
grown now so old and tough?

Essay

So many poems about the deaths of animals.
Wilbur's toad, Kinnell's porcupine, Eberhart's squirrel,
and that poem by someone—Hecht? Merrill?—
about cremating a woodchuck. But mostly
I remember the outrageous number of them,
as if *every* poet, I too, had written at least
one animal elegy; with the result that today
when I came to a good enough poem by Edwin Brock
about finding a dead fox at the edge of the sea
I could not respond; as if permanent shock
had deadened me. And then after a moment
I began to give way to sorrow (watching myself
sorrowlessly the while), not merely because
part of my being had been violated and annulled,
but because all these many poems over the years
have been necessary,—suitable and correct. This
has been the time of the finishing off of the animals.
They are going away—their fur and their wild eyes,
their voices. Deer leap and leap in front
of the screaming snowmobiles until they leap
out of existence. Hawks circle once or twice
around their shattered nests and then they climb
to the stars. I have lived with them fifty years,
we have lived with them fifty million years,
and now they are going, almost gone. I don't know
if the animals are capable of reproach.
But clearly they do not bother to say good-bye.

The Joy and Agony of Improvisation

There, the moon, just appearing
over dark pines, heavy and round,
the color of old parchment; and indeed
it seems archaic. What does it mean

in our histories, yours and mine,
except a myth no longer altogether
necessary, a theorem proven in another
millennium? This is a peculiar night,
uncomfortable. Well, it is like most moments
of the present, it doesn't fit us.
The low night wind, shifting, directionless,
moves the pine boughs, as if—so you say—
we were in the midst of voices in some
obscure contention. Of course we are.
But not obscure, only fruitless, stupid,
and very dangerous. Come,
let's go in the tent and sleep.

> Later
we waken, knowing the night has changed.
It's a high wind now. Strange how the voices
have turned to song. Hear
it rising, rising, then breaking, then
rising again, and breaking again. Oh, something
is unutterable, the song cannot reach it.
Yet we know it, know what we cannot
hear—out on the night's great circle,
the circle of consciousness with its far rim always
hidden, there where suffering and joy
meet and combine,
the inexpressible. How the song is striving
and how beautifully failing—the measure
of beauty, beyond plenitude,
never but always enough. Come
outside again, under tossing pines
and the racing clouds. This
is more than we could ever have meant
in our kiss; it is the gathering of our love
into all love, into that suffering and joy.
And see, up there in the sky, uncovered now
as the clouds stream away,
the moon,
so new, so clean and high and bright and true.

The Little Fire in the Woods

Even these stones I placed crudely once,
black now from many fires, bring me
a little knowledge, things I've done,
times endured, saying I am this one, this
person, as night falls through the trees. I see sand
darkening by the edge of an ocean, lights
on the rim of a galaxy, but I have not planned

my visions. I wish I could. We used birch bark
and spruce cones for tinder tonight, in which
a spark rambled until it met itself, flaring then
and leaping, throwing shadows among the trees.
Now punky gray birch smolders. Held
in the roots of our great spruce, I hold
my son, and the darkness thickens. It isn't

the cares of day I think of any longer.
True, I got this bruised belly when the machine
kicked this afternoon in our troubled potato patch
where the earth too cried out for justice,
justice! I tauten my muscles; the pain
is good and I wish it could be everything. But
larger errors are what we think of now

that have flared and leapt and thrown these shadows
of extinction among our objects. Or is the error
necessity, a circle closing? Son, in nature all
successions end. How long and slow is chaos.
Anywhere I am I see the slow surge of fire—
I, a diffraction, nothing. My son moves
closer. "Pop, how does the fire make heat?"

He does not see the fire I see, but I know
he knows a terror that children have never
known before, waiting for him. He knows.
Our love is here, this night, these woods, existing;
it is now. I think how its being
must emanate, like heat in conversion,
out beyond the woods to the stars, and how

it joins there in the total reckoning. It *must*.
Could anyone resist this longing all the time?
Oh, I know what I know, and I cannot
unknow it, crying out too for justice,
while the fire dwindles and shadows rise and flow.
But listen, something is here in the forest. Listen.
It is very clear and it whispers a little song:

> Sweet Bo I know thee
> > thou art ten
> and knowest now thy father is
> five times more again
> > and more
> and most gone out of rhymes
> sweet Bo
> > for thou dost know me
>
> And thou old spruce above us
> many are they of comrade and kin
> who love us
> > so that their loving proveth
> everything
> > although their way hath not
> the same compassion
> > as thy nonloving.
>
> Sweet Bo good night and hold me
> hold me close
> > the good firelight
> is dying
> > the woods are sighing
> and great is the dark
> > grateful
> am I for thee sweet Bo
> > good night
> good night.

In Memoriam

This warmish night of the thaw
in January a beech chunk
smoldering in my Herald
No. 22A box stove suddenly
takes fire and burns
hot, or rather I suddenly
who was reading the sweet
and bitter poems of Paul
Goodman dead last summer
am aware how my shed
becomes a furnace, and taking
my shovel I ladle
a great mush of snow
into the stove's mouth
to quieten it
and then step quickly
outside again to watch
the plume of steam rise
from my stovepipe straightly
and vanish into the mist.

The Mountain

Black summer, black Vermont. Who sees
this mountain rising nearby
in the darkness? But we

know it there. On the other side
in a black street of a black city
a man who is probably black

carries a Thompson
submachinegun, and don't
tell me how that feels

who carried one two years
in Italy; blunt-barreled power,
smooth simple unfailing mechanism

—the only gun whose recoil
tugs you forward, toward
the target, almost

like love. Separated
by this immense hill we share nevertheless
a certain knowledge of tactics

and a common attitude toward reality.
Flickering neon, like moonlight in beech leaves,
is fine camouflage. To destroy

can be beautiful.
I remember Mussolini's
bombed statues by the *dopolavoro* pavilion,

thick monsters transformed to elegance
by their broken heads and cut-off
arms. Let the city be transformed.

A man with a submachinegun is
invulnerable, the sniper's
sharp little steel or the fist

of a grenade always
finds him surprised. Hey,
look out, man! What you

trying to do, get yourself
killed? They're everywhere, everywhere,
hear?—the night's

full of them and they're looking
for a dead nigger—so watch it,
and go on fox feet and listen like a bat;

remember everything I told you.
You got to be smart enough
for both of us now.

But are you there? Are you
really there?

Essay on Stone

April abomination, that's what I call
this wet snow sneaking down day after day,
    down the edges of air, when we
        were primed for spring.

The flowers of May will come next week—in theory.
And I suppose that witty sentimentalist,
    Heine, saw this same snow falling
        in the North Sea

as into the Abyss. I look out now across
this pasture, the mud and wet matted grass,
    the waving billows of it, where
        the snow is falling

as into our own abyss. I stand on Marshall's
great rock, to which I have returned, fascinated,
    a thousand times, I stand as if
        on a headland

or on an islet in the midst of waves,
and what is this fascination, this cold desire?
    Once I wrote a poem about
        making love to stone

and a whole book in which the protagonist,
who was myself, carried a stone with him
    everywhere he went. I still like
        that poem and that book,

and yet for all my years of stone-loving
I've learned not much about stone. Oh,
    I can tell slate from quartz from sandstone—
        who couldn't?—and here

in this district we even have an exotic
stone, the talc, that feels warm and bloody
    in one's hand, but basically I am
        ignorant. Let

the geologists keep their igneous pyrites
to themselves. I don't even know if
    this great rock, projecting
        bigger than a barn

from the slope of the pasture, is a free
boulder that may have come here from the top
    of Butternut Mountain who knows
        how many eons ago,

or part of the underlying granite of Vermont.
I stand on its back, looking into the abyss.
    At all events the fascination
        is undeniable. I

always said there could be no absolutes,
but this is stone, stone, stone—
    so here, so perfectly
        here. It is

the abyss inverted, the abyss made visible.
Years ago when I wrote that other poem
    I might have taken pleasure from this,
        I think I would have. Now

I am fifty-three going on fifty-four,
a rotten time of life. My end-of-winter clothes
    are threadbare, my boots cracked, and how
        astonishing to see

my back, like that figure in Rembrandt's drawing,
bent. I shift weight on my walking-stick
    and the stick slips in wet lichen
        and then my boots skid too,

and down I go—not hurt, just shaken.
And what a hurt that is! Is it consoling
    to know I might have fallen
        into the abyss?

All this in silence, every word of it spoken
in my mind. The snow falls. Heine,
    there must be something wrong with us.
        I've heard this pasture

moaning at my feet for years, as you heard
that gray sea, we two shaken and always
      unconsoled by what we love,
         the absolute stone.

Valentine

That you should still send
yourself to me, that you should
arrive and attend like this
when there is no reason, when
actually there may be

contrary reasons, remains
the one phenomenon to me
most wonderful. Please,
lie back a moment, raise
your arm. I love to see

how the heart buries its
point in your groin, so dearly,
though it would be nothing
without its upward rounding
and flectioning over your

belly. Don't you believe
what you've been told, that now
valentines are grievous, all
the more for those as old
as we are? Still you come,

still you present this heart
with its swelling curves.
In wintertime I work
all night for quiet and then
go out to watch the dawn,

how February's bright stars
fade so that only knowing—
the mind—can tell they're there.
Strange that the light should be
a concealment. Yet I think

that's how it is with us, we
who are "enlightened," who know
sex and the hurt of sex,
yes, the era's learning, so
necessary. But still the older

and farther, farthest lights
shine behind the day, there
for our minds, or something
in us, to remember. Sweetly,
smilingly, when I come in

you throw the covers back,
an unconcealment, sending
from sleep your valentine
in the light the windows shed,
ice-laced, on your warm bed.

Once and Again

The peace of green summer lay over this meadow so
    deeply once
that I thought of England, cows lazy on the sward, the
    great elm
rising above them in diaphanous arches, the meadow
    that Marvell might have seen
from his study window but that I have never seen, yet I
    saw it
here. It *was* here, but that so long ago. And now the elms
of this region have mostly died, it is mid-November, the
    gray season,
purple on wooded hills, the meadow is gray and bare, the
    cows
are in their barn. I thought of England because so many
    things I love
have come from England, many images in my memory,
    although
I have never been there and have little hope that I will
    ever go.
I stand in the grayness, searching, looking for something
    without knowing what,
until I remember the great elm that used to be. To
    believe in the God
who does not exist is a heroism of faith, much needed in
    these times,
I agree, I know, especially since the hero is and must
    always be
unrecognized. But to love the God that does not exist, to
    love the love
that does not exist, this is more than heroism, it is
    perhaps almost
saintliness, such as we can know it. To discover and to
    hold, to resurrect
an idea for its own sake. Ah my heart, how you quicken in
    unrecognized energy
as hard little pellets of snow come stinging, driven on the
    gray wind.

Simple

Looking back 25 years I
    imagine it simple
(the reality being so
    uselessly complex),

how we made a pier, a jetty
    of lights, a brightness
in that fantastic dark,
    down which we took our way

to the vessel that lay in the
    shadows. We stood
a moment, looking here or there,
    and then you stepped aboard

as if this were perfectly
    natural, and I turned
back into the knowledge of going
    crazy from loneliness.

The lights went out, the pier
    vanished, the vessel
became a kind of legend
    of a ship beating

Oriental seas. Looking
    back I imagine
how I retired to a room
    I built, perhaps

a kiva lit by reflections
    of the moon, where I
celebrated over and over
    the trembling mysteries

of loss. I became a living
    brain in an effigy
of reeds and cloth and paint,
    completely insane.

John Dryden

Dry they call him, and dry is what he hopes
never to be, though springwater is all his drink
six nights after the welfare comes, and most
all his feed too, I sometimes think—though once
I saw him bring down a hare at seven rods
with a stone, and it didn't look lucky either.
When I asked him if he knew a famous poet
had the same name, he looked at me not quite
contemptuously; and yet I took a while to see
his scorn wasn't because he was smarter than I'd
credited—for a fact he can't read but about
half what's printed on the welfare check—but rather
because he'd been asked so damn many times before,
and he figured I should have known. I should have too.
Dry is not dumb. He's only crazy. Well, anyway
that's the general impression around the Plot,
which is what they call this section. My neighbor
rounds up her kids and locks her door when Dry
comes striding and caroling up the hill from town
in his outsize rummage pants with a carton
of grub held like an offering in both arms and his coat
gone slanty-wise from the fifth of sauterne
in his pocket. Paranoid, I'd say. There's more
than a few in these mountains, and sometimes I'm not
just certain about myself. But I know Dry.
I know he hasn't worked four consecutive days
on any one job in fifteen years. That's
indicative. Once we were haying up at Marshall's
and Dry took offense, we never knew what for,
and came after Marshall and me with his hayfork,
chasing us round the tractor, his face dead white
like snow that's thawed and frozen again; he did,
and it wasn't funny either. My kidneys ached
two hours after from thinking about that fork.
Finally he saw he couldn't catch us. He threw down
the fork and marched off, straight as a bee, over
the meadow, the pasture, the orchard, the fence, and was gone.
That year Marshall and I made the rest of the hay

alone. One time Gilbert told how he and Dry
were cutting sugarwood for old man Saunders
up toward Codding Hollow, and Dry took one
of his spells and came after Gilbert with the axe,
and Gilbert yanked quick on his chainsaw string and remarked,
"Dry, you damn fool, listen here—just you set down
that thing, or by the jumping Jesus Christ
I'll cut off both your arms." Dry set it down,
about three inches into a black birch stump, and marched
straight as a bee over brakes and brambles,
hobblebush and thornapple, and he was gone.
Which may be indicative too; he can be "took"
right sudden, but when he's licked he knows it.
And he's a fair hand at marching. He told me once
how it was here forty years back. "Them days
was cruel," he said, "awful cruel. Things was
turning on a slow reel"—and he made a motion
like so, like the bobbins down in the woollen mill
when they run half-speed. "Why, hell," he said,
"I had one of them five dollar gold certificates,
you remember? I felt like I was rich, and I was too,
but I spent it running some cunt. And it come back,
and I spent it again, and it come back again,
so help me over and over till the damn thing
wore itself out—I carried the pieces for years.
But they're gone now." One time Dry vanished,
clean gone, no one knew where and don't know yet,
but when he came back I met him up in the woods
and he stood on a spruce log and threw out his arms
and said, "God, Hayden, it's Moxie in the can,
being back on this here goddamn mountain again!"
And he laughed. The last what you could call steady
job Dry had, as far as I know, was 1945
down at the rendering plant in Burlington where he
slugged cows with an axe and pushed their guts
through a hole in the floor all day. "Stink? Jesus,
I guess I stunk! Like a she bear in whistling time,
but I made good money. Forty a week, and that
wan't bad in them days; but I spent it all
running the cunt, every dime. Why, I got
thrown out of five flea-bag rooming houses just

from owing the rent." Running's what we say
a bull does when you turn him out to pasture
with the cows, so you can see how Dry felt about that—
leastways providing you've ever seen a bull
in action. "But now, goddamn it"—Dry spit
and grinned sly-like with his uppers, which is all
the teeth I've ever seen him wear—"now
you could lay a slobbering big juicy one right there,
right there ready and open"—him leaning and making
a kind of slicing gesture along the log—
"and I couldn't do nothing, I couldn't touch it,
couldn't hardly spit on it," and he spit and grinned.
"It'd be all wasted, Hayden. I'm fucked, fucked,
and I ain't but fifty-nine—how old are you?"
That's Dry, that's him, the nailhead every time.

Well, he lives up in the old Connell sugarhouse now
that he's shingled all over with sap bucket covers
to keep the wind out, till it looks like a big tin fish
in the pines by the crooked brook, and there's plenty
more he could tell you, like how he got bit that time
by the cattle grub and took the "purple aguey,"
or how he has a buckshot in him that keeps going
round and round in his veins, catching him sharp-like
on his cotterbone when he don't expect it
every now and again, or how he eats forty aspirins
a day and hears sweet potato music in his ears,
or how he fell in a cellarhole at blackberry time
and landed on a bear—"I says, 'Whuff, old bear,
get you away from me,' and then I climm the hell
out of there"—or how . . . but have you noticed
I can't talk *about* him without talking *like* him?
That's my trouble. Somehow I always seem
to turn into the other guy, and Dry's the kind
that brings it out the strongest. But *his* trouble
is what I'm telling about now; for it's not
just buckshot in his blood, it's worse, a whole
lot worse. His reel is turning slower and slower,
no mistake. Crazy? I reckon he is. I sure don't
want to be there when he's took bad, even now—
if he's got a fork or an axe within grabbing distance.

But I'll go up to call on him in his sugarhouse.
I believe old Dry is preparing to march again,
or anyway preparing to prepare. And I believe
he'll go straight as a bee, white as a squall of snow,
knowing what he damn well knows, over
the goldenrod, the birchwoods, the pines and hemlocks,
over the mountain. And he'll be gone. And then
Marshall and I shall make this hay alone,
by God, and curse old Dry. But in our thoughts
we'll remember and remember how that man could march.

Johnny Spain's White Heifer

The first time ever I saw Johnny Spain was
the first day I came to this town. There
he was, lantern jaw and broken nose, wall-eyed and
fractious, with a can of beer in one hand and a
walkie-talkie in the other, out in front
of the post office. And I heard someone saying,
"Johnny, what in hell are you doing?" "I'm looking,"
he answered, in an executive tone, "for me goddamn
white heifer." "Run off, did she?" "Yass,"
he said. "Busted me south-side fence, the bitch—
if some thieving bastard didn't bust it for her."
"You reckon she's running loose on Main Street?"
Johnny looked down, then up, then sideways, or possibly
all three together. "Hell, no," he growled.
"She's off there somewheres." He swung his beer can
in a circle. "Me boys is up in the hills, looking.
I'm di-recting the search." Then he turned away
to a crackle on the walkie-talkie.
                          And that
was how Johnny liked it. He wasn't much
on farming, although his farm could have been
a fine one—closest to town, up on the hillside
overlooking the feed mill. But Johnny's curse
was a taste for administration. The "farm" was no more
than a falling-down barn, some mixed head
of cattle, and a flock of muddy ducks. Johnny
was the first man in the volunteer fire department
to have one of those revolving blue lights
set up on top of his car, and Johnny Spain
was *always* going to a fire. When he came down
off that hill of his in that air-borne '65 Pontiac—
look out! It was every man for himself
when Johnny was on the highway.
                          I used to think
sometimes I had a glimpse of that white heifer
that Johnny never found. "A goddamn beauty,"
he'd say. "By Jesus, she was. Why, I give
five whole greenback dollars cash and a pair

of Indian runners to Blueball Baxter for her
when she were a calf—there wan't a finer heifer
in the whole goddamn county." I'd see a flash
of white in the balsams at the upper end of the pasture
or in the thickets across the brook when I looked up
at twilight; but I never found her. Probably
all I saw was a deer-tail flashing.
                                        After
they changed the town dump into a sanitary
land fill operation the selectmen hired Johnny
for custodian, and they gave him a little Michigan
dozer to bury the trash with. Johnny loved it.
"Dump it over there," he'd holler. "Goddamn it,
can't you see the sign? Tires and metal
go on the other side." One time he even
inaugurated a system of identification cards,
so people from Centerville and Irishtown
would quit using our dump, and by God
you had to show your pass, even if Johnny
had known you for years. Part of the deal
was salvage, of course. Johnny could take
whatever he wanted from the accumulated junk
and sell it. Trouble was he mostly didn't
or couldn't sell it, so it wound up in his
barnyard, everything from busted baby carriages
to stacks of old lard kegs from the diner,
up there to be viewed by whoever cared to look.
And the one with the best view was Mel Barstow,
son of the mill owner, who lived on the hill
above the other side of town. There they were,
two barons above the burg, facing each other
at opposite ends, like the West Wind and the East Wind
on an old-time map. Mel had everything
he thought he wanted—a home like a two-page spread
in *House and Garden*, for instance, and a wife
that was anyone's envy, and a pair of binoculars
with which he liked to watch the gulls flying
over the river. Of course he'd seen Johnny's place
many a time, but one evening he focused down
on that barnyard, then quick got on the phone.
"Johnny, why in hell don't you clean up that mess

over there? It's awful. It's a disgrace." Johnny
didn't say much. But a couple of nights later,
maybe an hour past dark, he phoned up Mel.
"Mel," he said, "I got me a pair of them by-
nockyewlars over to Morrisville this forenoon,
and I been a-studying them goddamn birds out there,
and what I want to know is why in the hell
you don't tell that good-looking female of yours
to put some clothes on her backside when she's parading
up and down behind that picture window? Picture, hell—
I'll say it's a picture! It's a goddamn frigging
dis-grace, if you want to know the truth."
                                                            Well,
I expect for a while Mel's wife was the one
that would have liked to get lost, and maybe
Mel too, because it's a cinch you can't go down
to buy even a pack of Winstons at the IGA
without running into Johnny Spain, and of course
Johnny's the one that knows exactly, exactly
how to keep the sting alive, winking wall-eyed
both ways at once, grinning that three-toothed grin.

But Johnny Spain's white heifer was what was lost.
She wasn't found. Wherever she is, she's gone.
Oh, I'm not the only one who thought they saw her,
because reports kept coming in, all the way round
from the Old Settlement clear up to Mariveau's
gravel pit. But that's all they were, just
reports. She'd have made a first-rate cow,
I reckon, if a man could have caught her, only
of course somewhat more than a mite wild.

Marshall Washer

They are cowshit farmers, these New Englanders
who built our red barns so admired as emblems,
in photograph, in paint, of America's imagined
past (backward utopians that we've become).
But let me tell how it is inside those barns.
Warm. Even in dead of winter, even in the
dark night solid with thirty below, thanks
to huge bodies breathing heat and grain sacks
stuffed under doors and in broken windows, warm,
and heaped with reeking, steaming manure, running
with urine that reeks even more, the wooden channels
and flagged aisles saturated with a century's
excreta. In dim light, with scraper and shovel,
the manure is lifted into a barrow or a trolley
(suspended from a ceiling track), and moved
to the spreader—half a ton at a time. Grain
and hay are distributed in the mangers, bedding
of sawdust strewn on the floor. The young cattle
and horses, separately stabled, are tended. The cows
are milked; the milk is strained and poured
in the bulk tank; the machines and all utensils
are washed with disinfectant. This, which is called
the "evening chores," takes about three hours.
Next morning, do it again. Then after breakfast
hitch the manure spreader to the old Ferguson
and draw it to the meadows, where the manure
is kicked by mechanical beaters onto the snow.
When the snow becomes too deep for the tractor,
often about mid-January, then load the manure
on a horse-drawn sled and pitch it out by hand.
When the snow becomes too deep for the horses
make your dung heap behind the barn. Yes, a good
winter means no dung heap; but a bad one
may mean a heap as big as a house. And so,
so, night and morning and day, 365 days
a year until you are dead: this is part
of what you must do. Notice how many times

I have said "manure"? It is serious business.
It breaks the farmers' backs. It makes their land.
It is the link eternal, binding man and beast
and earth. Yet our farmers still sometimes say
of themselves, derogatively, that they are "cowshit
farmers."

2

        I see a man with a low-bent back
driving a tractor in stinging rain, or just as he
enters a doorway in his sheepskin and enormous
mittens, stomping snow from his boots, raising
his fogged glasses. I see a man in bib overalls
and rubber boots kneeling in cowshit to smear
ointment on a sore teat, a man with a hayfork,
a dungfork, an axe, a 20-pound maul
for driving posts, a canthook, a grease gun.
I see a man notching a cedar post
with a double-bladed axe, rolling the post
under his foot in the grass: quick strokes and there
is a ringed groove one inch across, as clean
as if cut with the router blade down at the mill.
I see a man who drags a dead calf or watches
a barn roaring with fire and thirteen heifers
inside, I see his helpless eyes. He has stood
helpless often, of course: when his wife died
from congenital heart disease a few months before
open-heart surgery came to Vermont, when his sons
departed, caring little for the farm because
he had educated them—he who left school
in 1931 to work by his father's side
on an impoverished farm in an impoverished time.
I see a man who studied by lamplight, the journals
and bulletins, new methods, struggling to buy
equipment, forty years to make his farm
a good one; alone now, his farm the last
on Clay Hill, where I myself remember ten.
He says "I didn't mind it" for "I didn't notice it,"
"dreened" for "drained," "climb" (pronounced *climm*)
for "climbed," "stanchel" for "stanchion,"
and many other unfamiliar locutions; but I

have looked them up, they are in the dictionary,
standard speech of lost times. He is rooted
in history as in the land, the only man I know
who lives in the house where he was born. I see
a man alone walking his fields and woods,
knowing every useful thing about them, moving
in a texture of memory that sustains his lifetime
and his father's lifetime. I see a man
falling asleep at night with thoughts and dreams
I could not infer—and would not if I could—
in his chair in front of his television.

 3

                              I have written
of Marshall often, for his presence is in my poems
as in my life, so familiar that it is not named;
yet I have named him sometimes too, in writing
as in life, gratefully. We are friends. Our friendship
began when I came here years ago, seeking
what I had once known in southern New England,
now destroyed. I found it in Marshall, among others.
He is friend and neighbor both, an important
distinction. His farm is one-hundred-eighty acres
(plus a separate woodlot of forty more), and one
of the best-looking farms I know, sloping smooth
pastures, elm-shaded knolls, a brook, a pond,
his woods of spruce and pine, with maples and oaks
along the road—not a showplace, not by any means,
but a working farm with fences of old barbed wire;
no pickets, no post-and-rail. His cows are Jerseys.
My place, no farm at all, is a country laborer's
holding, fourteen acres "more or less" (as the deed
says), but we adjoin. We have no fence. Marshall's
cows graze in my pasture; I cut my fuel
in his woods. That's neighborliness. And when
I came here Marshall taught me . . . I don't know,
it seems like everything: how to run a barn,
make hay, build a wall, make maple syrup
without a trace of bitterness, a thousand things.
(Though I thought I wasn't ignorant when I came,

and I wasn't—just three-quarters informed.
You know how good a calf is, born three-legged.)
In fact half my life now, I mean literally half,
is spent in actions I could not perform without
his teaching. Yet it wasn't teaching; he *showed* me.
Which is what makes all the difference. In return
I gave a hand, helped in the fields, started
frozen engines, mended fence, searched for lost calves,
picked apples for the cider mill, and so on.
And Marshall, alone now, often shared my table.
This too is neighborliness.

    4

                           As for friendship,
what can I say where words historically fail?
It is something else, something more difficult. Not
western affability, at any rate, that tells
in ten minutes the accommodation of its wife's—well,
you know. Yankees are independent, meaning
individual and strong-minded but also private;
in fact private first of all. Marshall and I
worked ten years together, and more than once
in hardship. I remember the late January
when his main gave out and we carried water,
hundreds and thousands of gallons, to the heifers
in the upper barn (the one that burned next summer),
then worked inside the well to clear the line
in temperatures that rose to ten below
at noonday. We knew such times. Yet never
did Marshall say the thought that was closest to him.
Privacy is what this is; not reticence, not
minding one's own business, but a positive sense
of the secret inner man, the sacred identity.
A man is his totem, the animal of his mind.
Yet I was angered sometimes. How could friendship
share a base so small of mutual substance?
Unconsciously I had taken friendship's measure
from artists elsewhere who had been close to me,
people living for the minutest public dissection
of emotion and belief. But more warmth was,

and is, in Marshall's quiet "hello" than in all
those others and their wordiest protestations,
more warmth and far less vanity.

5

He sows
his millet broadcast, swinging left to right,
a half-acre for the cows' "fall tonic" before
they go in the barn for good; an easy motion,
slow swinging, a slow dance in the field, and just
the opposite, right to left, for the scythe
or the brush-hook. Yes, I have seen such dancing
by a man alone in the slant of the afternoon.
At his anvil with his big smith's hammer
he can pound shape back in a wagon iron, or tap
a butternut so it just lies open. When he skids
a pine log out of the woods he stands in front
of his horse and hollers, "Gee-up, goddamn it,"
"Back, you ornery son-of-a-bitch," and then
when the chain rattles loose and the log settles
on the stage, he slicks down the horse's sweaty
neck and pulls his ears. In October he eases
the potatoes out of the ground in their rows,
gentle with the potato-hook, then leans and takes
a big one in his hand, and rubs it clean
with his thumbs, and smells it, and looks
along the new-turned frosty earth to fields,
to hills, to the mountain, forests in their color
each fall no less awesome. And when in June
the mowing time comes around and he fits the wicked
cutter-bar to the Ferguson, he shuts the cats
indoors, the dogs in the barn, and warns
the neighbors too, because once years ago,
many years, he cut off a cat's legs in the tall
timothy. To this day you can see him
squirm inside when he tells it, as he must tell it,
obsessively, June after June. He is tall,
a little gray, a little stooped, his eyes
crinkled with smile-lines, both dog-teeth gone.
He has worn his gold-rimmed spectacles so long
he looks disfigured when they're broken.

6   No doubt
Marshall's sorrow is the same as human
sorrow generally, but there is this
difference. To live in a doomed city, a doomed
nation, a doomed world is desolating, and we all,
all are desolated. But to live on a doomed farm
is worse. It must be worse. There the exact
point of connection, gate of conversion, is—
mind and life. The hilltop farms are going.
Bottomland farms, mechanized, are all that survive.
As more and more developers take over
northern Vermont, values of land increase,
taxes increase, farming is an obsolete vocation—
while half the world goes hungry. Marshall walks
his fields and woods, knowing every useful thing
about them, and knowing his knowledge useless.
Bulldozers, at least of the imagination,
are poised to level every knoll, to strip bare
every pasture. Or maybe a rich man will buy it
for a summer place. Either way the link
of the manure, that had seemed eternal, is broken.
Marshall is not young now. And though I am only
six or seven years his junior, I wish somehow
I could buy the place, merely to assure him
that for these few added years it might continue—
drought, flood, or depression. But I am too
ignorant, in spite of his teaching. This is more
than a technocratic question. I cannot smile
his quick sly Yankee smile in sorrow,
nor harden my eyes with the true granitic resistance
that shaped this land. How can I learn the things
that are not transmissible? Marshall knows them.
He possesses them, the remnant of human worth
to admire in this world, and I think to envy.

Crows Mark

They don't say gully, cove, cut, gulch,
glen, dell, etc., around here,
they call it a gulf, meaning
something less than a notch but more
than a ravine, and my house sits
in the bottom of Foote Brook Gulf. Back
about a hundred twenty years or so
the house was a barn, more like a shed,
a utility building
attached to a sawmill on the brook.
Well, all the mill that's left now
is part of the old foundation, but the shed
was converted into a house by tacking on a smaller
shed—I can show you where they toed in
the spikes through the two wall plates—
to serve as a kitchen. It still does.
The house is called Crows Mark. Don't ask me
why. I know, but I'm tired of telling.

It's a south-running brook, the Foote, rising
back up on the beaver meadows
on Butternut Mountain, which means
the Gulf runs north-south too,
roughly; and this in turn means the winter wind
that's usually more west than north sails
overhead—we hear it, a roar in the trees above,
but we don't feel it. Why, I've seen sheets
of snow flung over us, flopping and flapping,
and we dead calm underneath. Of course Marshall,
in his farmhouse up on the crest, gets it
full blast, so it's a good day's work to walk
from the house to the barn sometimes,
it seems as though. On the other hand,
still nights in winter the cold
spills down, over the pastures, the ledges,
into the Gulf till it's thirty-five
below on my thermometer, while Marshall
sits snug and comfy in the warmth

of the upper air where it's only twenty-five
under the zero, as I make sure
to point out to him next morning.
                              And then sometimes,
usually ten or twelve nights a winter,
the wind veers round due north, straight
down from the pole, and when it hits the Gulf
it's like full choke on a twelve-gauge
barrel—compression, you know what I mean?
I mind one time
in January—'sixty-eight, I think it was—
the wind blew the beam of my flashlight
twice around the maple by the woodshed
and wrapped it tight. You don't
believe me? Ask Marshall. The flashlight
was hanging there still next morning.
I let it stay till the batteries wore out
and it fell down.
                              Fortunately the wind
at Crows Mark sits mostly west by north,
through the Waterville notch, over our heads.

The Poet

All night his window
shines in the woods
shadowed under the hills
where the gray owl

is hunting. He hears
the woodmouse scream—
so small a sound
in the great darkness

entering his pain.
For he is all and all
of pain, attracting
every new injury

to be taken and borne
as he must take
and bear it. He is
nothing; he is

his admiration. So
they seem almost
to know—the woodmouse
and the roving owl,

the woods and hills.
All night they move
around the stillness
of the poet's light.

Essay on Love

Years. Many years. Friends laugh, including
even my best friend, Rose Marie, but they all
    are younger, and I might laugh as well
        to think how they will

come to know. Or tears might be as easy.
I used to drive this wedge in the maple blocks
        with pleasure; now I wouldn't care
            if I never saw another.

Yet the air so clear, utterly clear, and the blue
September sky arching the forest's bright crown
        so very deep: come, lean the sledge
            on its maple block

and walk away, slow, stepping by the little brook
where shad leaves turn coral and the turtlehead
        blooms, late this year, its petals
            still perfect and white.

See, ladies' tresses, right here where they always
were; kneel then to their fragrance, near
        to the cool of earth. And goldenrod,
            plumes of yellow

where yellow bees mumble, and asters, blue
and purple and white, New England asters
        that are our stars, and the small
            speckled asters, massed

at the edge of the clearing, that are called
farewell-to-summer; and there beneath them
        the peeping, deep, blue, shy eyes
            of the gentian,

so rare a color. Does that mean something? Count
the maple leaves if you can. Or those bluebirds
        perched, one by one, apart, on the wire
            over there, seven

blue in the sunlight: are they a rarity? Then
count too, as one always must, the "rare" pains,
        hernia raving, bladder and penis
            in an acid flame,

arthritic hip—was it Plato said a man
is finished at fifty-five? And Rose Marie,
        my dear friend, whose spine is a pain
            that I see marching

often enough in her young eyes. What do
the bluebirds say? They don't know why they wear
    that rare color, or why they gather now
        on that wire to fly

tomorrow to Guatemala; they don't know,
nor do I. Those seven little blue machines
    look down from their pain on a somewhat
        larger machine

of a somewhat less determinate color, down
into the clearing among coral shadblow leaves
    and the red and golden maple leaves
        and the parchment leaves

of moosewood, the speckled banks of asters.
Years, years; seasons and changes. Time,
    which is nothing but the measure of change—
        nothing, no meaning.

Years, years I've driven this wedge with my big
hammer into these maple blocks for Rose Marie,
    to keep her warm and give her stovewood
        for her kitchen

all winter, firesticks wrenched, split, pried
apart, each with the thought of her. I see
    so clearly, precisely, with the keen
        eyes of dispassion,

the trees, flowers, birds, all colors and forms,
but what good is such seeing in this chaos
    we used to call our order? She
        is invisible now,

a purity, the greater loveliness for the greater
seeing. Back to the block then, back once more,
    pick up the sledge, eyes down, and bend,
        bend to the labor

that is the only meaning. Farewell to summer.
Yes, let changes keep the time. I'll count
    no further, except these firesticks
        counted for her.

Missing the Bo in the Henhouse

In here, caught by the storm. How the rain beats
on the metal roof! And hens peck at my feet,

these my ladies, their mournful pessimism, ayie,
ayie, ayo, and my boy whom I have loved—how

shall I say it or sing it?—more than myself,
more than my poems (that are myself),

more than the world (that is my poems),
ladies, these thirteen years, and now

he is turning, turning away. I know
we are "carried about the sun," about and about,

this conglomeration, a higgeldy-piggeldy
planet, incomprehensible, I could not

be part of it. And I am.
Carried. Desire long ago beaten out,

so that I wanted small things only, a song,
a boy. No, it will not cohere, this "world";

relentless the years and it will not. Mind
cannot make it. Ladies, do you know ever

what it means to be carried? Woe, ladies,
the boy is turning. A current runs on the grass.

And the dark falls early. Come now, up to your roost
and let the evening dance begin, the slow sarabande—

aft by fore, or aft by aft, which
shall it be?—turning, turning in the cadence

of your song. Ayie, ayie, ayo. Slower
and slower. Good night, ladies,

in your hurtling house. The time of the mouse
has come, the rain strums on your roof.

Keep close and keep warm. Bless me if you are able,
commend me to the storm. Good night, good night.

Paragraphs

1

Begin right here. The Campground Road. Some calls it
    the
Hogback, but that's up higher. Down here's the river.
And there's Vermont, all ridge and valley
and all cockeyed—seem'z'o. Over
acrost is the hayth-o-land, Whiteface and all,
Madonna, Mansfield. Butternut's back here. And Baldy
Langdell's uncle's place was right there,
him that set his house as square
as his own square Yankee head afore he died   and Baldy
    died and old
Jimmy   and Hank Rago
King, Malcolm, Jackson and all—
    all in a breath of years.
                    A cold wind,
                        old and cold,
sprung these waterdrops from a bare birch bough,
these lightdrops scattering to the edge
of a pool of darkness. Or say we could glimpse
    Vivaldi's parchment now,
his hand flinging down a bright arpeggio . . .

2

Keep going. *There's nothing else to do.* Past
the few farms remaining, Manchester's, Jones's.
Past brutishness new since last
I drove here, sliced stone,
eviscerated hills. And then the worst,
these superadded trailers, this prefab, damned fashion
out of Monterey or Bronxville, God knows where—
the national mean taking over. Or
the mean nationals.
                    Keep going, Waterville
to Johnson. I'd have thought
(almost) this was too tough, they couldn't spoil it,
ridge and riverbottom, massed heights,

granitic Vermont.　　　But they've walked on Kailas
　　　and thrown
town dirt on snow-bright Sati,
　　　they've exulted
before Kali.　　　They've put their feet on the moon.

　　3
Ithiel Falls, below the Nazarene campground. A name
clinging to its old place. The falls were blown out
in a WPA so-called work program,
1934 I think, to avert
another flood like '27 that had been true bedlam,
death-night all over Vermont. Icy water, the flame
in the lungs. God!
　　　　　　　Yet the dynamite
was a fool's work, wasted. What
caused the flood was a jam in the fall's crest,
where the old covered bridges,
floating loose on high water, came to rest,
creating a dam. But then the new bridges
that replaced them were ironwork. Could *they* float?
Ah, Ithiel Falls, lovely cascading down ferny ledges,
and I never saw it.
　　　　　　　Why were the falls blown out?

　　4
Why was the passenger pigeon exterminated?
　　　　　　　　　　　　Sometimes
I dream of those bridges; downriver on the flood,
shapes in dark water, awash and lumbering.
Why did the beatitude
who shot the last otter in Otter Creek come home
bragging? I dream how they yawed and stumbled,
how they wallowed almost but not quite like the huge
Jurassic animals caught in the deluge.
Why were the braves castrated, the stretched squaws
bayoneted up their vaginas?
Bridges are only bridges, that's all, bumping along,
　　　spandrel and truss,
post, brace, beam—
　　　　　　arks

of a minor people and a time too small for grief,
crunching, foundering, gone in the rain-drenched dark.
I grow old, my dreams are factual and brief.

   5

Not night now. Dawn. Six o'clock, a November morning.
But raining still. I stop. In the blown falls the river
sinks on a long grade, curling
through the dogleg. I lower
my window. Rain hisses on the coarse snow remaining
from yesterday's freeze where broken stems of mullen
fence the ditch. A grove of popples,
grayish-green, is a drabness opposite,
with one stark white birch outstanding. A jay,
slanting tidily across the water
to a low branch, jeers as he goes. Way away,
way in the East, beyond our boarded up
Nazarenes, the sun struggles in a fog.
                              Once at Walden
it was the "morning star" calling us to the order
of this world.
           Tell me   Henry David   are you still called?

   6

The Lamoille River Valley otherwise known
as these objects jays trees snows that wont cohere
or where on the waters of darkness Apollyon
stalks to make this hour
dawn's awful madness in the Valley of Humiliation
and him the Angel of Death but Im no Christian
and first becomes last coherence fails
connections cherished 50 years and all's
lost no art more Ill write what I want how I want
dont bug me about my words
the vision is cold chaos and I need what warmth
my old mind knows I rub my beard
I crank my window closed but there there the Prince of
       Prose
Apollyon water-marcher his terrible swift regard
flinging look his icy pointed oldwords where he goes.

7

Arthritic gray snowlight hobbles down the valley
        westward.
It is day. Who also will choose my delusions and bring
my fears upon me? Engrafted words
I sing and sing and sing
upon blocky objects floating downriver, my days, while
        my godhood
ordains resolutions, a chaos of light, of flood,
a *catastrophe*. I turn the key, ram
the old truck in gear, and grind home
down the Campground Road toward the colorless, futile
dawn—past Farrell's,
up Stearn's Hill, past the Whiting Lot. More trailers,
earth crumbling and eroding visibly
beneath the snowcrust, pines and birches massacred. I
        feel
nothing but cold. I catch my reflection on the wet
        window, alone,
a face old and broken, hunched over Ixion's wheel.

                ·   ·   ·

8

the one called Next steps up
to the wall. a face detailed
and well remembered. but
my voice won't call
when i try it. stuck. i shut
my eyes. i hear the gunbolts
slide home. i open
my eyes. my hands
are missing. i reach.
i have nothing but wrists.
the face falls down. i retch.
the next one is called Next.
so dream after dream they keep
going. yet i'm sound awake.
the world has gone to sleep.

                ·   ·   ·

9

It was the custom of my tribe to be silent,
to think the song inwardly, tune and word
so beautiful they could be only held,
not sung; held and heard
in quietness while walking the end of the field
where birches make a grove, or standing by the rail
in back of the library in some northern
city, or in the long dream of a tower
of gothic stoniness; and always we were alone.
Yet sometimes two
heard it, two separately together. It could come
nearby in the shadow of a pine bough
on the snow, or high in the orchestral lights,
or maybe (this was our miracle) it would have no
intermediary—

                a suddenness,

                    indivisible, unvoiced.

           .   .   .

   10

"There was this girl   18, 19   and slight
the way they are in that country   (you know)   laying
by the others in the ditch   taking
the bullets
with her body/   with which she shielded
as best she could   both her little child
and her zillion-year-old grandmother"
                      hic divisio
facta est inter Teutonicos et Latinos
Francos   circa 843 a.d./
              or,
                ahi serva Italia
di dolore ostello—
Dante who made it all ours and even more terrible
than perhaps it was   eloquence
so grave and so sweet.
         "Her mouth was narrow
blood-choked/   we thought her eyes widened
more in incredulity than pain . . ."
                  Ahi
       thou inn of sorrow.

           .   .   .

11

Oh I loved you Pete Brown. And you were a brother
to me Joe Marsala. And you too sweet Billy Kyle.
You Sid Bechet. And Benny Carter.
And Joe Jones. Cozy Cole.
Cootie Williams. Dicky Wells. Al Hall. Ben Webster.
Matty Matlock. Lou McGarity. Mel Powell. Fats Waller.
Freddie Green. Rex Stewart. Wilbur & Sid
de Paris. Russ Procope. And Sister Ida
Cox dont forget her. And Omar Simeon. Joe Smith.
Zutty Singleton. Charlie Shavers.
Specs Powell. Red Norvo. Vic Dickenson. J.C. Higginbotham.
Nappy Lamare. Earl Hines. Buck Clayton.
Roy Eldridge, Pops Foster. Johnny Hodges. Ed Hall.
Art Tatum. Frankie Newton. Chu Berry. Billy Taylor.
And oh incomparable James P. Johnson.

                    Brothers I loved you all.

                 .   .   .

12

I was watching the telly not serious you know just looking
with my wife there too and feeling all right after a dinner
at home together for once with our own cooking
and afterwards a whiskey for sipping
and I really was feeling all right   Almost shocking
when you consider my age (65) and my line of work
(political) but even in the Trouble
you forget sometimes/you have to   The doorbell
sounded/Jenny bringing that big memo
to sign for the early pickup
I opened   It was a hooded man with a pistol
He fired three times/there was a terrific
thud and I stood there watching a huge wall subside
under the pendulum stroke of a ball   while my wife's
      hysterics
drifted down the street like a shower of rain/
                          And then I died.

                 .   .   .

13

And the water/the rising water

                                             nothing like it

     for force

moving everywhere   embracing every obstacle

          as if it were love

              carrying everything before it/

                                a miracle

of conversion

                      See how it spreads out & across

the field

              making a nacreous sky-reflecting lake

                where geese

         in thousands

rest for four days

          on the long journey to Hudson's Bay

Rills rivulets streams springs ditches pools

                  it's a watery world

all trace of the old order going fast/

                      it spills

              mud and the rich mould

        of its long astonishing suppuration

                       and then

it's over

     all at once the movement has come full

and everyone

        puts on shirts of bright triumphant green.

             .   .   .

14

In filthy Puerto Rico there lives a bird with no
legs and transparent wings, a somewhat small
bird whose flight is awkward and slow
yet it spends its whole
existence in flying. Luckily it knows how
to ride high currents above the eagles, hawks, crows
and all the preying host that seeks
its life continually. As long as it keeps
above them, soaring between them and the sun,
it cannot be seen, partly
because the predators are blinded by the exceeding shine

of brightness, partly because the heart
of the bird is the only thing that shows, a speck
in its transparency. High it flies, flies, flies, hungry and hurt,
until at last it falls forever on filthy Puerto Rico. And the
     name of the bird is blank.

       .   .   .

    15

"I am a fanatic lover of liberty, considering it
the unique condition in which intelligence, dignity,
and human happiness may develop and grow;
not the purely formal liberty
conceded, measured out, and regulated by the State,
an eternal lie which in reality represents
nothing more than the privilege
of some founded on the slavery
of the rest; not the individualistic, egotistic,
shabby and fictitious liberty
extolled by the school of J.-J. Rousseau and the other
schools of bourgeois liberalism,
which gives us the would-be rights of all men
as embodied in a State that limits the rights of each—
an idea which leads inevitably to the reduction

    16

of the rights of each to zero. No, I mean the only
kind of liberty that is worthy of the name,
liberty that consists in the full development
of all the material, intellectual, and moral
powers which lie hidden in every person; liberty
which knows no restrictions beyond those
determined by the laws
of our individual natures,
which cannot properly be regarded as restrictions
since they are not imposed,
but are immanent and inherent, forming
the very basis of our material, intellectual,
and moral being—they do not limit us, they are
the real and immediate conditions of our freedom."
—Thus living light cast back from a burnt-out star.

       .   .   .

17

RAVAGE, *v. t.* To lay waste; to subject
to depredations; to work havoc or devastation upon;
to sack; plunder; despoil. *Syn.*—
RAVAGE, DEVASTATE, SACK
agree in the idea of despoiling or laying waste.
Ravage emphasizes the idea of violence: *devastate*,
that of waste or ruin; *sack*,
that of plunder or pillage. One *ravages*
or *devastates* a country, one *sacks* a town.

Unquote.

Please/
distinctions are important. There's still one man
who chooses with care. Anyone who agrees
may love me or not, but those condemning
my methods never will.

Regard the breeze
how it plucks bright autumn leaves
          one after another
                    to expose the timber.

18

And so with paragraphics.

It was in summer
that lovely word chosen with care when I
first loved this valley where the river
was a curving ribbon of sky
lacing together the fields of every color
potatoes timothy mustard alfalfa clover
and purple widemarching corn. The farms
lay scattered in their places, a barn,
a house, fenced fields irregular. Their old
horse-drawn mowers
and manure spreaders rusted in the yards. Fold
within fold the darkening hills arose
toward glowing mountains. Here was a peacock, there
a Mongolian pheasant—no exotics, no more
than the useless horse or ox, for this was where

all things lay in nature, even the plastic flowers,
the flowering plastics,

                  the plastic farmers . . .

                     Wordsworth!

thou should'st be living in this hour:
Vermont hath need of thee /

                 Carruth

being at all events not up to it;

               the ancient power

of that vision is gone.

           Gone? Was I bemused? The scars

are not new, the macadam was here then,
half the forests lay in slashed ruin,
the river's blue was more likely not sky
but the paintworks in Hardwick
cleaning its vats again. And yet

               somehow

it *was* absorbed,   humanity sick
with greed, with loathing, somehow was taken in
by earth, water, mountain . . .

             No more! The weak

have conquered and the valley is their domain,

ugly, evil, dying. The old soft lines,
knoll and glen, mountain and river, that held
the farms like poems curled in time,
have been ripped out,

         raveled,

wrenched apart. The connections gone. It was dynamite
did it

    more than chainsaws or the great Cats, but—

        ahi

           it was men's minds

that did it!

       In this town, Johnson,

some have sold their own and everyone's
birthright to the ravagers, on our east and our west,

and particularly these two:
André Tournailler (*Anglice,* Toenailer) and Jacob Blesh.
Yes, townsmen, friends, I name *you,*
Andy and Jake, against every rule of Yankee decorum,
I name you in your public guilt. Here and now.
Look, the trailer park, filling station, plastic ranches,
      the rural

21

slums par excellence that were your farms! And all
for a hot pocketful of dollars.
                         I don't say others
haven't done as much, Farrells, Hills,
Berrys, Lahouillers, Parkers,
and so on—the length of the valley, to Hyde Park, Morrisville,
Wolcott, Hardwick, or westward to Lake Champlain,
a shambles, ravaged, devastated, gone,
or going fast.   All in the name
of "development." But good friends, where are your dollars
now? And who has profited?
Not farmers. Not (God knows) poets. None of us. The poor
play patsies again for mean-spirited
weaselly downcountry men, the capitalists, varmints
come ravaging in our dooryard like the strange coyotes
come from the west.
         And your *best* is what you gave them,
                     o my friends—
            your lives, your farms.

22

Now tell me if we don't need a revolution! Black
is the color of my only flag/
                     and of man's hope.
Will revolution bring the farms back?
Gone, gone. The only crop
this valley will grow now is the great landwrack,
breakage, erosion, garbage, trash, gimcrack.
We burn it. The stink trails in the air,
a long thin smoke of floating despair
down the time of our valley. Someday we will be free,
someday when it's too late.

It's true, the real revolutionary is one who can see
all dark ahead and behind, his fate
a need without a hope: *the will to resist.*
The State is universal, the Universe is a state.
Now ask me if I am really an anarchist.

                    .   .   .

    23
Another hard, hard morning with a hard snow
Falling small and fast. It is eight below.
Yet the ash pail brims. I must go
Out to the garden and sow
This remnant of value where the beans will grow
Next summer maybe. The goddamned gods bestow
And men . . .
                    are at best a paradigm
Sowing and reaping in the void of time.
Or say that one must do what one does as though
It might mean something, so—
Broadcasting ashes, swinging my shovel low,
Spreading this color that I don't know,
Dirty lavender, dirty pearl, row upon row,
Death upon death, "sowing the ashes," to and fro,
A *tour de force* in an abandoned studio.

                    .   .   .

    24
And I was past caring   so many, too many men,
so many children /   body broken, slack
as the spirit   skin & bone
like a burlap sack
with a litre of rice in the bottom.

                               No one
wants lugging that around,
                    let the others run,
I said, and sat right down, there
where I was, and looked up into the air
to see it coming.
                    And when it came (that spout
of flaming jelly)   I cursed
and then I made a great sound: no shriek, no shout,
more like an enormous croak—the worst
I had ever heard.

For once then   *once*   I knew
what I had done was the most
                    and maybe the first
human thing I had ever been permitted to do.

·   ·   ·

25

Reading myself, old poems, their inside truth that was
(is, is!) crucial, tree stark in lightning glimpse, hidden
mostly by the storm: complexities,
modes, names, manners,   words laden
with terror. What true voice? Where? Humiliated, in throes
of vacillation, roundhead to cavalier to ivy league to smartass—
never who I was. Say it plain:
death/beauty, loneliness/love, wisdom/pain,
they the simple coordinates. Was it shameful
to be insane, or so grotesque
to wrench lucidity out of nowhere? Yet my call
came a whisper, my sentence an arabesque,
my song falsetto. Put the book back on the shelf.
Gone goodness. Dear mother, dead father, what burlesque
of feeling phonied us, that made you make me hate myself?

·   ·   ·

26

A day   very solid   February 12th, 1944
cheerless in New York City
                    (while I kneedeep
elsewhere in historical war
was wrecking Beauty's sleep
and her long dream)
                    a day (blank, gray) at four
in the afternoon, overheated in the W.O.R.
Recording Studios. Gum wrappers *and* dust
and a stale smell. A day. The cast
was Albert Ammons, Lips Page, Vic Dickenson,
Don Byas, Israel
Crosby, and Big Sid Catlett. (*And* it was Abe Linkhorn's
birthday.) And Milt Gabler
presided beyond the glass with a nod, a sign. Ammons
counted off
                    a-waaaaan,,,   *tu*!

and went feeling
his way on the keys gently,
                    while Catlett summoned

    27
the exact beat from—
            say from the sounding depths, the universe . . .
When Dickenson came on it was all established,
no guessing, and he started with a blur
as usual, smears, brays—Christ
the dirtiest noise imaginable
                    belches, farts

                              curses

but it was music
                music now
                    with Ammons trilling in counterpoise.
Byas next, meditative, soft/
                    then Page
with that tone like the torn edge
of reality:
            and so the climax, long dying riffs—
groans, wild with pain—
and Crosby throbbing *and* Catlett riding stiff
yet it was music   music.
                        (Man, doan
fall in that bag,
            you caint describe it.)
                        Piano & drum,
Ammons & Catlett drove the others. *And* it was done
and they listened *and* heard themselves
            better than they were, for they had come

    28
high above themselves. Above everything, flux, ooze,
loss, need, shame, improbability/   the awfulness
of gut-wrong,   sex-wrack,   horse & booze,
the whole goddamn mess,
And Gabler said "We'll press it"   *and* it was "Bottom Blues"
BOTTOM BLUES   five men knowing it well   blacks & jews
yet music, music   high

in the celebration of fear, strange joy
of pain: blown out, beaten out

                         a moment ecstatic
in the history
of creative mind *and* heart/   not singular, not the rarity
we think, but real and a glory
our human shining, shekinah . . .   Ah,
                 holy spirit, ninefold
I druther've bin a-settin there, supernumerary
cockroach i' th' corner, a-listenin, a-listenin,,,,,,,
        than be the Prazedint ov the Wuurld.

FROM If You Call This Cry

a Song (1983)

Words in a Certain Appropriate Mode

It is not music, though one has tried music.
It is not nature, though one has tried
The rose, the bluebird, and the bear.
It is not death, though one has often died.

None of these things is there.

In the everywhere that is nowhere
Neither the inside nor the outside
Neither east nor west nor down nor up
Where the loving smile vanishes, vanishes
In the evanescence from a coffee cup
Where the song crumbles in monotone
Neither harmonious nor inharmonious
Where one is neither alone
Nor not alone, where cognition seeps
Jactatively away like the falling tide
If there were a tide, and what is left
Is nothing, or is the everything that keeps
Its undifferentiated unreality, all
Being neither given nor bereft
Where there is neither breath nor air
The place without locality, the locality
With neither extension nor intention
But there in the weightless fall
Between all opposites to the ground
That is not a ground, surrounding
All unities, without grief, without care
Without leaf or star or water or stone
Without light, without sound
                              anywhere, anywhere . . .

I Tell You for Several Years of My Madness I Heard the Voice of Lilith Singing in the Trees of Chicago

1

Of waste and again of waste, and of the waste of wasting, o void,
  o desolation:
of the cruelty of the seed, of the unbearable force of the seed,
  o sinking sun:
of the vessel shattered and the vessel cast away, o oblivion.

2

Before the weak sister Eve who betrayed the serpent that had lived
  at peace in my cave, there I was:
before the strange sister Inanna who destroyed the *huluppu*-tree
  for a place to lie dreaming of Gilgamesh, there I was:
before the rushing and circling of the winds of the desert, yes,
  before God, there I was.

3

In the blink of the eye of the black crow in the center of the
  leafless tree:
in the knot of the wood of the tree, the knot ever unblinking:
in the potsherds broken in their brightness, scattered and shining
  beneath the furious sun.

4

For I was bitten, for I bear the insignia of the toothmark on my
  shoulder:
for I was thrown down and compelled to carry the sands of the earth
  in my womb:
for I was sold for a song, bought for a tablet of law, and my
  compassion was made my indenture.

5

How long, beside the waters, beside the moonlight, beside the stone:
how long, at the hot edges of highways, both the eastern and western:
how long, where the sewers foam and the black bayous rot.

6
Because my body resembled the wheatfield, they tilled it:
because my breasts were like the blossoming apple boughs, they
    broke them:
because the animal of my sex was wild in fugitive mystery, they
    tamed it for servitude.

7
O Batseba, who opened her knees to an harpist and took God's
    scorn for the song's sake:
O Batseba, who opened her knees to an hero and took man's pity
    for the deed's sake:
O Batseba, o beautiful and wise, o traitorous sister.

8
A woman's bone is bright as the tree of the olive in sunlight:
a woman's flesh is beat down like the unripe fruit:
a woman's death lies gleaming and twisted like a torn-out root in the
    early morning dew.

9
Therefore the awakened bird cries once in the night:
therefore the sweet fire sings when it reaches the knot:
therefore, o therefore Lilith her cry, and Lilith her curse and her
    detestation, and again I sing: *therefore*.

On Being Asked to Write a Poem Against
the War in Vietnam

Well I have and in fact
more than one and I'll
tell you this too

I wrote one against
Algeria that nightmare
and another against

Korea and another
against the one
I was in

and I don't remember
how many against
the three

when I was a boy
Abyssinia Spain and
Harlan County

and not one
breath was restored
to one

shattered throat
mans womans or childs
not one not

one
but death went on and on
never looking aside

except now and then like a child
with a furtive half-smile
to make sure I was noticing.

Anima
(for *Janet*)

There she was. While the flare
of the August sky darkened
and twilight deepened, deepening
the field, while the evening star
came holily out, she tended
the fire by the edge of the woods,
a young woman both dark and fair,
moving among these natural
things, the fire, the woods, the star,
and the distant mountains, barefoot
and wearing a sweatshirt, a skirt
that fell loosely over her thighs,
she who was strong in her sex,
with her hair loosened, a figure
of sturdiness in the female way,
bending as she stirred the beans
in the blackened pot or walked
in darkening grass with a bucket
on her hip or split firesticks
with her axe; and I saw a scene
of ten thousand years ago or maybe
ten thousand to come; and she also
must have thought of time, for she
pointed to the star, and her voice
was distinct on the twilit air,
"Look at the star now, look
at a thing that was always there."

I do look. And I see her, and she
is there. Others too, her husband,
Rose Marie and the Bo; but for one
moment, or forever, I see only her,
her and the star and the fire
and the woods and the mountains,
a pure moment from an existence
in the other consciousness where time
is stilled and no fear is felt.

Firelight and starlight and woman,
complete and beautiful, for only
one place is known, ever, and this is
there, meaning beauty, meaning
all that is human in one fathoming,
the passion of mind, the reflectiveness
of spirit. I do not know, on this shore
of a shadowed field in the shadow of my
old age, what else a man lives for.

The Point

In a broken
mirror you might
lie fragmented

a nipple paired
with an eye
and all your parts

strange in their
new arrangements.
And I might take

these fragments (if I
were so given)
in these selfsame

chances
and cement them
to that sunniness there

of morning wall
where you would be
a mosaic of your

random beauty.
Glittering
you would endure

for years and years
in time that will admit
no chances.

But the point is you
you looking out
a little unknowable

not wanting to be known
not in that way
not like a chance

but holding your own
like time   like stone
like leaping flame.

TWO ROMANTIC PIECES

"Une Allée du Luxembourg," by Gérard de Nerval

There now. She's passed, that slight
One, just there and gone like a bird,
Holding a bright flower, humming
Some tune I almost heard.

Might she have loved me? Maybe
Hers is the last little light
In the whole world that could enter
My dark, darkening night.

But no. That time is over.
Good-bye, small light that shone,
Fragrance, woman, music,
Happiness . . . you are gone!

"Tristesse," by Alphonse de Lamartine

Once more let me go, I said, where that blest shore
Images Naples over an azure sea,
Palaces, hills, unmisted stars, the orange trees
Blossoming there under skies eternally pure!
What delays you? Come! I would see again
Vesuvius flaming, mounting from the very waves;
On her heights I would worship the inchoate dawn;
I would descend, as in a smiling trance, those slopes,
Leading the way for somebody I adore.
Follow me where the coast of that tranquil bay
Winds in and out; let us tread once more that path
Our footsteps knew so well, to the ruined Gardens
Of Cynthia, Virgil's Tomb, the Temple of Venus:
There, under orange trees, under the flowering vine
That twines so slenderly amidst the myrtle
And weaves a mantle of blossom above your head,
In the music of gentle waves or the murmuring wind,
There together, alone with our love, alone in nature,
Like the light our life will seem sweeter.

Now

My days resemble the torchlight, acrid, guttering,
Little by little snuffed in the winds of anguish,
Or shedding sometimes, when in my heart the memories
Of you rekindle, a lurid and momentary glimmer.
I do not know if finally the gods will permit me
To complete my difficult journey here on earth;
My horizon contracts, and my bewildered eyes
Hardly dare search beyond one narrow season.
    But if I must die tomorrow,
If in this land once destined for happiness
    I must let fall from my hand
    The goblet that fate had seemed
To wreathe with rose petals fragrantly all
For my pleasure, I beg them only to lead me
Again to the shore that your memory still adorns.
There in a sad remoteness I may hail once more
Those sunny vistas, and die where I tasted life!

Regarding Chainsaws

The first chainsaw I owned was years ago,
an old yellow McCulloch that wouldn't start.
Bo Bremmer give it to me that was my friend,
though I've had enemies couldn't of done
no worse. I took it to Ward's over to Morrisville,
and no doubt they tinkered it as best they could,
but it still wouldn't start. One time later
I took it down to the last bolt and gasket
and put it together again, hoping somehow
I'd do something accidental-like that would
make it go, and then I yanked on it
450 times, as I figured afterwards,
and give myself a bursitis in the elbow
that went five years even after
Doc Arrowsmith shot it full of cortisone
and near killed me when he hit a nerve
dead on. Old Stan wanted that saw, wanted it bad.
Figured I was a greenhorn that didn't know
nothing and he could fix it. Well, I was,
you could say, being only forty at the time,
but a fair hand at tinkering. "Stan," I said,
"You're a neighbor. I like you. I wouldn't
sell that thing to nobody, except maybe
Vice-President Nixon." But Stan persisted.
He always did. One time we was loafing and
gabbing in his front dooryard, and he spied
that saw in the back of my pickup. He run
quick inside, then come out and stuck a double
sawbuck in my shirt pocket, and he grabbed
that saw and lugged it off. Next day, when I
drove past, I seen he had it snugged down tight
with a tow-chain on the bed of his old Dodge
Powerwagon, and he was yanking on it
with both hands. Two or three days after,
I asked him, "How you getting along with that
McCulloch, Stan?" "Well," he says, "I tooken
it down to scrap, and I buried it in three
separate places yonder on the upper side

of the potato piece. You can't be too careful,"
he says, "when you're disposing of a hex."
The next saw I had was a godawful ancient
Homelite that I give Dry Dryden thirty bucks for,
temperamental as a ram, too, but I liked it.
It used to remind me of Dry and how he'd
clap that saw a couple times with the flat
of his double-blade axe to make it go
and how he honed the chain with a worn-down
file stuck into an old baseball. I worked
that saw for years. I put up forty-five
run them days each summer and fall to keep
my stoves het through the winter. I couldn't now.
It'd kill me. Of course, they got these here
modern Swedish saws now that can take
all the worry out of it. What's the good
of that? Takes all the fun out, too, don't it?
Well, I reckon. I mind when Gilles Boivin snagged
an old sap spout buried in a chunk of maple
and it tore up his mouth so bad he couldn't play
"Tea for Two" on his cornet in the town band
no more, and then when Toby Fox was holding
a beech limb that Rob Bowen was bucking up
and the saw skidded crossways and nipped off
one of Toby's fingers. Ain't that more like it?
Makes you know you're living. But mostly they wan't
dangerous, and the only thing they broke was your
back. Old Stan, he was a buller and a jammer
in his time, no two ways about that, but he
never sawed himself. Stan had the sugar
all his life, and he wan't always too careful
about his diet and the injections. He lost
all the feeling in his legs from the knees down.
One time he started up his Powerwagon
out in the barn, and his foot slipped off the clutch,
and she jumped forwards right through the wall
and into the manure pit. He just set there,
swearing like you could of heard it in St.
Johnsbury, till his wife come out and said,
"Stan, what's got into you?" "Missus," he says,
"ain't nothing got into me. Can't you see?

It's me that's got into this here pile of shit."
Not much later they took away one of his
legs, and six months after that they took
the other and left him setting in his old chair
with a tank of oxygen to sip at whenever
he felt himself sinking. I remember that chair.
Stan reupholstered it with an old bearskin
that must of come down from his great-great-
grandfather and had grit in it left over
from the Civil War and a bullet-hole as big
as a yawning cat. Stan latched the pieces together
with rawhide, cross fashion, but the stitches was
always breaking and coming undone. About then
I quit stopping by to see old Stan, and I
don't feel so good about that neither. But my mother
was having her strokes then. I figured
one person coming apart was as much
as a man can stand. Then Stan was taken away
to the nursing home, and then he died. I always
remember how he planted them pieces of spooked
McCulloch up above the potatoes. One time
I went up and dug, and I took the old
sprocket, all pitted and et away, and set it
on the windowsill right there next to the
butter mold. But I'm damned if I know why.

Marvin McCabe

First off, I have to say I can't talk good.
What's the use of saying it? Damned if I know;
nobody could miss it. But something always makes me
try to apologize. The talk machine's busted,
that's all. Connections all screwed up. Have you ever
wondered how it would be to have your thought
that's clear and shiny inside your head come out
like a mouthful of mud? As for simple things,
I say, "Ahwan ahg' abah'"—what does it mean?
I say it five times, "Ahwan ahg' abah',"

grimacing and smiling, *pleading*, and no one
hears me say I want to go to the bathroom.
I have to take a leak, for Christ's sake!—what
could be simpler? Well, for me, almost everything
if it doesn't require speech. That's why I have to
rely on Hayden. He's listened to me so much
he knows not only what I'm saying but what
I mean to say, you understand?—that thought
in my head. He can write it out for me. What
I'm thinking now—and most of the time—is how
I wish whoever invented beer had been stuffed
back and smothered in his mother's womb. That's
damn-fool wishing, of course. But it's the kind
a man in my fix can spend a lot of time on.

It was hard at home. I mean hard. We never
had a farm. Lived here and there, my old man
milking cows for other farmers or shoveling gravel
on the road gang; he did most anything. But what he was
was a trader. He'd go up to Canady looking
for auctions, in Knowlton or around Granby,
and he'd buy a team or a set of chairs or a
barrel full of old dishes or God knows what,
and he'd bring the stuff home and sell it. He'd
do it all right, I'll give him that; he was a
damn good trader—I never knew but one man that
took him in a deal. Yet he never made any
money, not to speak of. He was a *trader*—
do you understand what that means? It's a breed,
a special kind of a man, I think, or like some
craving or craziness in the head. Pa had it.
And he figured his boys should have it too.
It was the only way he could see that a man
might get somewhere; one good deal could set it
off, he thought, and then a couple more—no saying
how far a man could go. He used to tell us
how John D. Rockefeller started out peddling oil
door to door in a wagon. With me it was blankets.
One morning, the winter I was twelve, Pa hitched
our nag to the old sled and piled a dozen blankets
on behind. "Get going," he said, "and don't you

show your face till you've sold them." I did it.
Took me four days and three rotten freezing nights,
but I did it. And what I minded most wasn't
the selling or the cold, it was driving that horse
and that lousy sled. Somehow that stood for Pa,
as if he himself was standing there behind me,
sounding off in my ear. But I drove that horse
many a time more before I was through with it,
selling whatever Pa loaded on behind, junk
mostly.
       So you can see how I felt when I
turned sixteen and got my license. I felt
free. I was like a prisoner stepping out the door
of the jailhouse for the first time. I bought a car,
a wreck but I made it run, and I drove it
all over the countryside. And then of course
I discovered beer. All kids do, but can you
imagine what it meant after peddling away
my childhood behind that horse? The first time
I put a couple bottles of Bud inside me
it was—wow, terrific. That buzz, like something
I dreamed of. Happiness. Christ, what a miracle,
I was free and happy too! Who could have foreseen
anything like that? Then I got a job, I got
a girl, I got her pregnant, the usual story
here in the mountains, I was married at seventeen,
and when the war came I went across and got
shot up—the usual story there too. What matters
is what came next: another car, a dark night,
a bellyful of beer, and that sharp turn on Rt. 15
just east of the gravel pit. I wish I'd died.
But they put a plate in my skull and pinned my arm
together with little bits of silver and wire,
and a year later I remembered who I was.
Marvin McCabe—I could hardly believe it.
That was twenty-eight years ago. I believe it now.
Marvin McCabe is a slobbering idiot: he talks
like one, so he must be one, mustn't he? And he walks
like one too, shuffling along with his cane.
Anyone who thinks the important part of his brain
is the part that thinks—well, let him take a look.

No, it's the part that controls the tongue and the other
motor functions. And mine's seventy-five per cent
dead.
            My wife was gone before I got back from the
hospital, gone and remarried—naturally. And I
had nothing to say about it, and wouldn't have said
anything if I had. But there's been no woman
for me in twenty-eight years; that's hard to take.
My boy used to come out to see me regularly
once a week, on schedule, which was a mistake,
of course, but one he rectified himself
when he was fourteen and ran away. I think
he ran off just to escape those afternoons
with me. For hours he'd sit there and say absolutely
nothing; but his looks would speak—how he despised me.
Naturally, and that was hard to take too.
And Pa, he despised me, and still does, old
as he is, though we've lived together this whole time.
He talks to me just like he talks to the dogs,
and when I try to answer he cuts in, "Shut up,
shut up that mumbling, no one can understand it."
When people come he tells them, "Look at me,
eighty-five years old and I'm looking after
a fifty-year-old man. Marvin's not worth
keeping, he's no good for nothing." And I just
smile. That's hard to take, believe me. But the hardest
of all was always this feeling that my thoughts
were shut inside me, that all I could *do* was smile.
I knew the words but couldn't say them—do you
see what that means? *No one knew who I was.*
It was like those people who believe your soul
can pass into another body when you die.
I was in the wrong body, but I hadn't died.
Can jail be worse than that? I wanted to die.
I would have if wanting could do it. But then
I came to see it doesn't make any difference.
If I spoke, what would it do?—my thoughts mean nothing,
my life means nothing, my death means nothing.
And everything means nothing. Sometimes I sit
here in this bay window and look out
at the field, the hills, the sky, and I see the boulders

laughing, holding their sides and laughing,
and the apple trees shaking and twisting with laughter,
the sky booming and roaring, the whole earth
heaving like a fat man's belly, everything
laughing. It isn't because we're a joke, no,
it's because we think we aren't a joke—that's
what the whole universe is laughing at. It makes
no difference if my thoughts are spoken or not,
or if I live or die—nothing will change.
How could it? This body is wrong, a misery,
a misrepresentation, but hell, would talking make
any difference? The reason nobody knows me
is because I don't exist. And neither do you.

Bears at Raspberry Time

Fear. Three bears
are not fear, mother
and cubs come berrying
in our neighborhood

like any other family.
I want to see them, or any
distraction. Flashlight
poking across the brook

into briary darkness,
but they have gone,
noisily. I go to bed.
Fear. Unwritten books

already titled. Some
idiot will shoot the bears
soon, it always happens,
they'll be strung up by the paws

in someone's frontyard
maple to be admired and
measured, and I'll be paid
for work yet to be done—

with a broken imagination.
At last I dream. Our
plum tree, little, black,
twisted, gaunt in the

orchard: how for a moment
last spring it flowered
serenely, translucently
before yielding its usual

summer crop of withered
leaves. I waken, late,
go to the window, look
down to the orchard.

Is middle age what makes
even dreams factual?
The plum is serene and
bright in new moonlight,

dressed in silver leaves,
and nearby, in the waste
of rough grass strewn in
moonlight like diamond dust,

what is it?—a dark shape
moves, and then another.
Are they . . . I can't
be sure. The dark house

nuzzles my knee mutely,
pleading for meaty dollars.
Fear. Wouldn't it be great
to write nothing at all

except poems about bears?

My Meadow

Well, it's still the loveliest meadow in all Vermont.
I believe that truly, yet for years have hardly

seen it, I think, having lived too long with it—
until I went to clean up the mess of firewood

left by the rural electric co-op when they cut
my clump of soft maples "threatening" their lines,

this morning, the last day of September. My maple leaves
were spilled in the grass, deep crimson. I worked

with axe and chainsaw, and when I was done I sat
on my rock that had housed my fox before the state

executed him on suspicion of rabies, and then
I looked at my meadow. I saw how it lies between

the little road and the little brook, how its borders
are birch and hemlock, popple and elm and ash,

white, green, red, brown, and gray, and how my grass
is composed in smooth serenity. Yet I have hankered

for six years after that meadow I saw in Texas
near Camp Wood because I discovered an armadillo

there and saw two long-tailed flycatchers
at their fantastic mating dance in the air.

Now I saw my meadow. And I called myself all kinds
of a blind Yankee fool—not so much for hankering,

more for the quality of my looking that could make me
see in my mind what I could not see in my meadow.

However, I saw my serviceberry tree at the edge
of the grass where little pied asters, called Farewell-

to-Summer, made a hedge, my serviceberry still limping
from last winter's storms, and I went

and trimmed it. The small waxy pointed leaves
were delicate with the colors of coral and mallow

and the hesitating blush of the sky at dawn.
When I finished I stepped over my old fence

and sat by the brook on moss sodden from last night's
rain and got the seat of my britches wet.

I looked at my brook. It curled over my stones
that looked back at me again with the pathos

of their paleozoic eyes. I thought of my
discontents. The brook, curled in its reflections

of ferns and asters and bright leaves, was whispering
something that made no sense. Then I closed my eyes

and heard my brook inside my head. It told me—
and I saw a distant inner light like the flash

of a waterdrop on a turning leaf—it told me
maybe I have lived too long with the world.

Song: So Often, So Long I Have Thought
(for Cynthia Tokumitsu)

So often, so long I have thought of death
That the fear has softened. It has worn away.
Strange. Here in autumn again, late October,
I am late too, my woodshed still half empty,
And hurriedly I split these blocks in the rain,
Maple and beech. South three hundred miles
My mother lies sterile and white in the room
Of her great age, her pain, while I myself
Have come to the edge of the "vale." Strange.
Hurrying to our ends, the generations almost
Collide, pushing one another. And in twilight
The October raindrops thicken and turn to snow.

Cindy stacks while I split, here where I once
Worked alone, my helper now younger than I
By more years than I am younger than my mother—
Cindy, fresh as the snow petals forming on this old
Goldenrod. Before her, it was war-time. In my work
I wondered about those unarmed Orientals swarming
Uphill into the machine guns, or those earlier
Who had gone smiling to be roasted in the bronze
Cauldrons, or the Cappadocian children strewn—
Strewn, strewn, and my horror uncomprehending. Were they
People, killers and killed, real people? In twilight
The October raindrops thickened and turned to snow.

I understand now. Not thoughtfully, never;
But I feel an old strange personal unconcern,
How my mother, I, even Cindy might vanish
And still the twilight fall. Something has made me
A man of the soil at last, like those old
Death-takers. And has consciousness, once so dear,
Worn down like theirs, to run in the dim
Seasonal continuance? Year by year my hands
Grow to the axe. Is there a comfort now
In this? Or shall I still, and ultimately, rebel,
As I had resolved to do? I look at Cindy in the twilight.
In her hair the thick October raindrops turn to snow.

A Little Old Funky Homeric Blues for Herm

Knock off that hincty blowing, you Megarians,
I got a new beat, mellow and melic, like
warm, man. I sing of heisty Herm.

'Twas early dawn when somebody smashed the stars
and hardnose Herm was born. He lay there
on his cot a while, then he raised up and said:

"Ma—" that's Maybelline "—Ma, who's my daddy?"
"Him!" snorted Maybelline. "Yeah, but who is he?"
"He come in a white cloud." "Hah, I knows the kind—

them so big-balled." "Gully-low he was,
sure enough." "He live up Sugar Hill?"
"Up some hill somewheres, that's all I know."

"I knowed it!" And hero Herm he laughed
and looked in the glass and smarmed to hisself:
"An eight-rock mama and a ofay pop—

hey, man, you got something coming sure!"
Then the window flashed with curious light.
"Ma, ma, what's that?" "Why just a car going by."

"Car—what kind of car?" "Hmm, it look like a
Jaguar." Horrid Herm flaked out in a fake of sleep,
but then rose up, unseen, and out the door,

down the dark hall where he found a rusty pipe
which cried out, "No, no! I too am an object of this world!"
But hectic Herm he said, "Bah, you nothing now."

And he killed it with one blow, and bent it,
and then and there, all by himself,
invented the tenor sax. O hippocrene Herm!

He blew, he strutted, he made the walls fall down
and then fall up again, with only 96 bars
of Hermetic Swan-shaped Blues; and bowed and departed.

Down the stairs, down the block, past fizz and fuzz
—"You mess with me, baby, I bite you ass"—
down Fifth, and down and down, till there it stood,

the great red Jag tethered tight outside
the pad of Apollonio. Apollonio the brave,
fair, friend to all, talented, liberal, who played

all day on his symphony orchestra.
Hoodoo Herm he fingered the secret switch,
and drove that Jag like a fist of fire

across the park, up Amsterdam, to a cave
on Morningside Heights. Wham!—it was hidden.
Hieratic Herm sat down and pulled his pud,

and then and there, all by himself, invented
man's sacrificial relationship to fate.
Twelve times he jetted to the twelve prophets in order.

Handsome Lake
Simon Kimbaugh
John Wilson
André Matswa
Muana Lesa
Kanakuk
Marcus Garvey
Enoch Mgijima
Wodziwob
Doctor George
Isatai
Makandal

And bowed, and said, "I done what you told me."
Then home, and slipped through the keyhole
in the form of a flatted seventh. Back to the cot.

Maybelline cried, "Where you been, child?"
But holy Herm: "Nowheres. How you expect
a little newborn baby going to go?"

Then Maybelline looked wise: "Little fucker,
I knows you. The day that big man
from up yonder stuck his thing in me

he got a heap of trouble on the world."
Then hijacker Herm he snuggled in his rildy
and answered: "Ma, you is quaker oats. Now listen,

ain't you heard about status yet? It's like powerful,
like being on top, but with class, no sweat, see—
and I aim to get me some. If nobody—

meaning that mister big on the hill—
give it me, I gets it any way, that's all,
any way I can. Don't you worry none, I

blowing real sharp on this gig already."
And he fell asleep. Snuffling and snoring.
Then came the fuzz with Apollonio

to wake him up. "Boy, where'd you stash that Jag?"
"Jag?—Jag?—I don't know nothing about—"
but Apollonio lifted him and shook him hard,

and here's where handy Herm did his cleverest,
for he farted juicily inside his diaper
and topped it with a sneeze. Awed Apollonio

dropped him like a toad. Yet at last
they agreed to submit the matter to
the man on the hill, who smiled when he heard

of heretical Herm and the big red Jag,
smiled and said: "You got to give it back."
And haunted Herm said: "Shucks," and he said:

"Dadgumit," but what could he do?—
something tied his tongue. He was like a child,
he *was* a child. He had to give it back.

So haywire Herm and affable Apollonio
trucked down the avenue together,
until, after a ways, Herm unslung his horn,

the golden tenor, and with a groan and a squeal
bopped out the changes of Cora Banty's Ride,
and Apollonio's blond wig stood up

and he jigged, he twitched, he chuckled, and he perspired,
and at last he leaped and cried: "Oh, man, I dig you,
teach me to play that thing." "What!"

said hispid Herm, "you grunch and groan!
You dirty them fingers so lily-white!"
"I got to, man, I got to. Give me that beat again,"

cried Apollonio, down on his knees and rocking.
"What it worth to you?" "Anything, anything—
take my Jag, take my electronic wristwatch,

I got to have that horn. Oh Herm, we are brothers now."
And so hilarious Herm went home again,
grinning and gloating. But Maybelline

she said: "You too big for you britches, boy,
they going to fix you yet. Prince of Thieves
they calls you. Maybe you is and maybe you aint

but you know what they going to make you?—
Prince of Storekeepers, that's what, Prince
of Nickels and Dimes, Prince of Gouging and Niggling,

you going to be a rat just like them, little prince,
you hear?—squeezing and scrambling and squawking
just like them, just like them,

and the very best name they ever going
to call you is Psychopompos."
"Shit," said homunculus Herm.

The Cowshed Blues

Exsurge, gloria mea;
exsurge, psalterium et cithara

Intro

    Intent in the
    night in the
    cone of light
      writing

Vamp

    Or what's called
      writing
    though words must come
    throb by throb
        through the membrane
    of the great black drum

16 bar theme

    It was a cowshed when he took it
    a one-cow barn beside a brook
    in a cove of alder and birch

    floor of plank and rank urine, the wooden
    stanchel worn in a cow's long wintertimes
    heavy   with animal woe

    in the back wall
    was a hole
    with a board flap
    hinged on a harness strap

    where they shoveled through
    the manure
    onto the manure pile
    once in a while

    so he made a window where the hole was
    a table and a stove, and sought the grace
    words give for love in a writing place

Piano break
>Light on the page and all else
>the raging dark

12 bar theme
>And tonight the shed rides free and the cove
>its alders and birches
>falls downward among the stars

>because intensity does this, a mind
>out of time, out of place—
>body a field of forgotten wars

>and making does this, the breakthrough
>to a great beat throbbing
>in a place without place

>o moment, moment   pure
>he is an undetermined existence
>part of eternity, gone in inner space.

Stop-time chorus, trombone
>Soaring
>>on the modes
>>of sound
>the modulations

>moving
>>over and through
>>the pulses
>of his love

>known by no name now
>>although
>>a muse of everlasting
>voluptuousness is aware of him

>and the particular
>>tones follow
>>one another
>freely   inexorably

Scat chorus

    Cow now . starflow . the slow
    beat . over and over . flies .
    ow . the cords . the blood
    urine and dung . how
    flying . chains in the neck of
    hathor . perpetual beating .
    her womb . beating . hot eyes .
    now . beating . a great flying .
    and pain . and beating . now

Two choruses ad lib, trumpet

    What our people have never known
    but always felt
    in the mystery of the word

    is a force
    contained but not expressed
    spoken and unexplained—

    for meaning falls away
    as the stars in their spirals
    fall from the void of creation

    how simple and how necessary
    this discipline! which is the
    moment added to moment of being

    movement added to movement
    notes in the throat of the horn
    being and being and being

    dying, born   and he
    is alone, free
    creator of what he cannot help but be

Vamp, guitar and bass
    "Holiness," he says
      hearing an unexpected
    modulation:
          at the point of flow
    always this beat, this beat
      repeated
    instant of everything he knows
      now   forever   existing   here
    it must
      be holiness

Out-chorus
    And blues is also
      a crying in the night
    exhaustion, constriction
      in the cone of light

    and he looks up sighing
      to the dark glass
    where looking back at him
      is his father's face

Stop-time bridge, clarinet
    All's fallen back
      back
    collapsing into time
      time

    the beat   of the great drum   is going
      going
    in the wind in the trees
      in the wind in the trees

Ride out, half-time
    It is   his face now
    his own   his
      and old in a moment
      miseries, histories

    his and his father's
    reflected   little things
      among others of this earth
      the alders and the birch

Tag, drums
>   But the beat remains
>   the moment of purity somewhere
>   poised on its long
>>   flow   far out, far in

Tutti
>   or on this page fallen
>>   notations   of remembered song.

Almanach du Printemps Vivarois

Am I obsessed by stone? Life has worn thin here
     where the *garrigue* slopes down to the fields,
to the *vignes* and *luzerne*. A meager surface
     covers the stone—stone so long my own
life and my song—only gray tufts of grass, moss,
     the thyme just beginning in its rough
tangles to glitter with little purple blooms,
     the summer savory so very
fragrant now, the *piloselles*, the broom, the first
     poppies and thistles, with no more than
a few *cades* and *chenes verts*, scrubby and prickly,
     to make shadows; yes, a sparse surface
and the stone shows through, flakes, grits, fragments, sharp shards
     littering the ground, or the outcrop
of smooth bedrock here and there, and then the huge
     escarpment across the way, looming
over the valley. The stone gleams, pale gray. Life
     has worn thin here, washed always down. Ah,
republica de miseria, so sang
     one poet in the olden tongue, *lo*
lenga d'oc, a song of dole, and he meant it
     to be taken hermetically
both ways, of spirit and body; *trobar clus*
     for the oppressed and loving people.
Now one tractor, small in the distance, rumbles
     below in its *sulfatage*, spraying
the vine-rows, while nearby a wall that someone
     a couple of hundred years ago
assembled, the stones chosen with care, all flat
     and set tight with the top row upright
and angled, has fallen, sprawled away. Only
     parts of it remain to exhibit
the original construction. Life has worn
     thin here, and mine as well. A cuckoo
calls, calls, calls, damned mad invariable sound,
     over and over, telling the mad
impossible hours. *Lo cinc d'abrièu,*
     lo cocut deu chantar, mòrt o vièu.

And who can ignore such meanings, messages.
      intimations? A squawking magpie
staggers through the lower air, a jerk and a
      joke. Time flies. But murkily and in
confusion, cock-eyed. Yet it's mid-morning, mid-
      April, the Ardèche, one might do worse,
one might do almost immeasurably worse,
      and the sun at last is strong after
our long shivering in the *mistral*. Jacket
      and sweater are pillow now, I'm down
to my shirt, my companion already down
      to practically nothing, lovely
to see, and although I am content to bake,
      eating the sun (as the Italians
say) to put marrow in my bones while I make
      lazy words run in a lazy song
about stones, she is all business and she knows
      her business—oh, nothing could be more
plain, she in the lotus position, her board
      propped on her knees. She draws. She is young,
she has a right to be serious. Finches
      are serious in the oak-bushes,
chittering, chattering, gathering gray grass
      and gray lichen for their nests. Finches?
They look more or less like finches. Ignorance—
      how it invades a petulant mind
aging in laziness and lust. And the sun,
      higher now, stronger, a radiance
in the sky and a blaze in the valley's faint
      blue mist, burning on the stone, turning
our Ibie white, our river so greenly fresh
      three weeks ago, now gone dry as bone,
is hot, hot, blessedly hot, stirring my blood,
      warming me through, and also moving
the summer savory to even greater
      fragrance, the plant called *sariette*, known
as an aphrodisiac. Do I need that?
      Not after last night. Strange, the seed still
sprouting in hot sun from the hill of stone. Strange,
      the old spirit and old body still
flouting time and murk and confusion in lust.

The young woman in her sunhat and
underwear peers off at the distance, then down
        at her page, so certain of her work,
its newness, its autonomy—her art there
        darkening the paper. But my song
is old, my stone song; I patch it up from shreds
        of Latin grandeur and trobar rhyme,
old, conventional, wrong—who knows it better?—
        though all conventions are old as soon
as they occur. They are always occurring.
        The song is all in my head. Shreds of
culture. Confusions of time. It is noon now,
        my shirt goes to the pillow, I look
at my own white skin, almost parched it seems, creased
        with age-lines. And it gleams! Suddenly
the republic of misery is blazing,
        the old stone is glowing, and as if
at a stroke of some cosmic tone everything
        falls silent, the finches, the tractor,
the cuckoo, the wax crayon squeaking, even
        the small wind in the grass, yet nothing
has stopped. Am I deaf now too? Or is silence
        the indispensable analogue
of brilliance? And stone is silent. Ancient stone,
        glowing stone. Song in its confusions
is all extraneous, it dies away. Shreds
        of time. In April when the seed sprouts,
in the Ardèche huge with silence where life is
        thin, an old man and a girl are held
in stillness, in radiance, in flames of stone,
        for the moment of eternity.

Mild Winter

Mid-December but still the ground's unfrozen, taking
my impress receptively, as if it would pull me in.
The snowfall melts wherever it finds warm earth
but clings to everything aboveground, twigs, leaves, stems,
debris of the woods floor. It is a tracery
under the trees, a damask. Behind me my boot-tracks
are a clumsy soilure. Beside me little snow crystals
make arabesque on the bark scales of an old spruce,
filigree on the ear-like petals of lichen. Somewhere
in the trees ahead a raven rises and moves away
and at once in my mind dark wings labor. I peer
through gray air but the raven is not visible; only
a voice is there, guttural bad news penetrating
the thickness of spruce trees. No wonder cousin Edgar
chose a raven to be his metaphysical bird,
though he was wrong to give it no more than that silly
word to say; ravens are articulate, like the whole
race of pessimists, speaking in many tones. I too
have had my Ligeia, I have had my Annabel Lee.
A web of snowflakes brushes my forehead, I hear
the United Farmers milk truck gear down and rumble
on Schoolhouse Hill, but Edgar, cousin, you died
twelve years ago now when we were forty, and I've
outlived you, somehow I've left you, and I'm
changed, so sober in these damp northern woods.
I wonder will anybody remember to tell my wife
she can draw on my social security when the time
comes? The raven will. I hear him muttering far off,
his voice now, with the voices of the others, very soft
yet lucid across gray air. In my mind black shapes
settle and shift and rise and settle again, talking
in the spruces. Strange how their words, so quiet and remote,
come distinctly over the distance, like words in dreams.
Idiot ravens, take off—depart! You should have been long gone
to the southern misty garbage-laden rivers! I always
said if the winter must come then let it be cold,
let it be bitter and pure and silent, not like this.

Who Cares, Long As It's B-Flat

Floyd O'Brien, Teagardens Charlie & Jack
     where are the snowbirds of yesteryear?

Boyce Brown, Rod Cless, Floyd Bean
     Jimmy McPartland, Danny Polo
Hank Isaacs, Davy Tough, Jim Lannigan

     where are you, Jim Lannigan?

Jesus but you were awful musicians
     Pee Wee, Abby, and you Faz
awful awful. Can you please
     tell me the way to Friar's Point?

"Aw, Jess." "Shake it, Miss Chippie, but don't
     break it."
"Listen at that dirty Mezz!" Can you
     tell me please
the way to White City? Where
     can I find
the Wolverines, Teschemacher?

     Leon Rapollo?

Eubie, Punch, Darnell? "Cut him
     Mister Reefer Man." "I wisht
     I had a barrel of it."

Muggsy, Muggsy where art thou
     where is Pine Top
where are the Yanceys now?

   35 years
     swish-swish of a velvet cymbal
     twinkling leaves
  in the lilac tree

"When I die
     when I die
          please bury me

sweet mamo
     in a sardine can . . ."

Coda
  And these little cats think
    they discovered something

       (gawd

damm)

Moon-Set

The dark will come, I said,
soon now at moon-set.

And I looked and looked to see
our night-lady

so grave and magnanimous
go away

over our hill, smiling
a moment, no more, through pointed

spruces; and the dark came,
the snow turned gray.

Yet then slowly the gray
was silver, the snow-clad

spruces began to sparkle,
and even the frost of the air

was illumined, a slow
mazy

dance of light-specks. I
looked overhead

to the stars, suddenly
so present, so much a part

of the night. The night,
I said, is all grave

and all a dance and never
dark. And on my slow

snowshoes I danced and skipped
gravely down the meadow.